To

Aunty Joan +
Uncle Alan,

I hope this book encourages
you to come and visit Newcastle
again very soon.

Lots of Love from

[signature] Christmas 2005

Newcastle upon Tyne

Text by Steve Newman
Photography by Graeme Peacock

SANDERSON BOOKS LIMITED
NORTHUMBERLAND

Opposite: The Swirle Pavilion, Quayside

The authors would like to thank the following for their generous help and support, without which the production of this book would not have been possible:

Cindy Balderston (Eldon Garden Shopping Centre)
Peter Bowden (D.T.Z.)
Iris Boyd (Newcastle upon Tyne City Council, Press Office)
Dr Ian Brunt (City Carillonneur at the Edith Adamson Carillon, Civic Centre, Newcastle upon Tyne)
The patient staff at the Central Library's Local Studies Centre
Co-operative Insurance Society for permission to use the photograph of the Central Arcade)
Very Rev'd Christopher Dalliston (Newcastle Cathedral)
Leila d'Aronville (Sage, Gateshead)
Howard & Jenny Dawe
Wendy Dawley (Newcastle Airport)
David Denham (Senior Markets Inspector, Newcastle upon Tyne City Council)
Gemma Diduca (Metro Radio Arena)
Jane Donnelly (Lord Mayor's Principal Secretary)
English Heritage
Fenwick Ltd.
Great North Eastern Railway
David Gregory (Eldon Square)
Dorothy Hadden
Alison Hesselberth (Newcastle upon Tyne City Council)
Land Securities (The Gate)
Barry T. H. Mason (M.W.E. Architects)
Steve Mclean (Hancock Museum)
Greg Miller (Theatre Royal)
The National Trust
Newcastle upon Tyne Hospitals NHS Trust
Newcastle United Football Club
Alan Newton (Central Pub Company)
Bob Nicholson (Hanro Developments)
Derek Osborne (Collins & Stewart, Milburn House)
The staff at the Ouseburn Resource Centre
The Ouseburn Trust
Dr. Mark S. Pearce (University of Newcastle upon Tyne School of Clinical Medical Sciences (Child Health)
Eric Smith (Church of St. John the Baptist)
The Society of Antiquaries
Margaret Souter (Newcastle Tourist & Information Centre)
Philip Thirkel (Victoria Tunnell)
Alison Tombling (Schools and Community Liaison Officer, Nexus)
Andrea Trainer (Northumbria University)
The Master, Brethren and Staff of Trinity House
Jonny Tull (Tyneside Cinema)
Tyne & Wear Museums Service
David Williamson (Newcastle Race Course)
David Wilson
Paul Wappat, Ian Robinson and listeners of B.B.C. Radio Newcastle's Blue Bus Show
Michael Young

First published in Great Britain in 2005 by Sanderson Books Limited.

Text and photographs copyright Steve Newman, Graeme Peacock and Sanderson Books Limited; 2005
The moral right of Steve Newman and Graeme Peacock to be identified as the authors of this work has been asserted in accordance with the Copyright, Designs and Patents Act of 1988.

ISBN 09548024-1-1

Text by Steve Newman / www.stevenewman.co.uk
Photography by Graeme Peacock / www.graeme-peacock.com
Designed by Sokell Design / www.sokell.com
Editor: Catherine Bowen
Printed and Bound in Italy.
Set in Frutiger

Half-title page: The Civic Centre Carillon Tower
Title page: The Swirle Pavilion, Quayside

Other titles published by Sanderson Books Limited:
'Holy Island of Lindisfarne'
'Northumberland'

Sanderson Books Limited
Front Street, Klondyke, Cramlington
Northumberland, NE23 6RF

Newcastle upon Tyne

The City

INTRODUCTION

This book is not intended to be a history of Newcastle upon Tyne, neither is it a portrait of the city, it is best described as a celebration of the forces that have gone before and are happening now that will shape the city in the future. All cities must evolve and grow to survive, Newcastle has had its growing pains, adolescent traumas and perhaps even its midlife crisis in the nineteen sixties.

Newcastle is a city built on valleys and steep ravines, strip away the concrete, steel and tarmac and something akin to a relief map of the Cheviot Hills would appear. This is what gives the city its character and charm, today we can still walk up some of these river valleys but mostly we walk on top of them, little realising the streams they held still run beneath our feet, now incorporated into the city's drainage systems. In some cases even the bridges that previous generations walked over still survive.

It is the buildings of Newcastle that make this city so unique, its sweeping streets and narrow medieval lanes sit side by side with soul-less concrete monstrosities, beautiful timber framed houses and modern cathedrals of steel and glass.

These buildings hold many surprises. It is a failing of most human beings that we hardly ever look up when walking, yet Newcastle is a glorious city of turrets, domes and clocks. What mysteries do these buildings hold? Who is the lady on the Northern Goldsmith's clock? Who are the ships' figureheads

on the corner of the Bigg Market and Grainger Street? And perhaps the greatest mystery of all, what exactly is the vampire bunny doing in St. Nicholas' Churchyard?

In researching for this book I have walked hundreds of miles around the city's streets, so much so that the map I once took around with me is now firmly implanted in my head, as are a host of other memories. Whenever I stopped for a while, scratching my head looking for a street, building or statue, I would immediately be accosted by a citizen of Newcastle offering their help.

Invariably, when I explained that I was researching for a book on Newcastle a torrent of information would come out, in particular I remember the three council workers who were cutting the grass at the Hancock Natural History Museum who told me about the Victoria Tunnel.

What also came out was an intense pride in Newcastle upon Tyne, virtually everybody I met described it as 'Our City'. This may be because Newcastle is relatively compact and you can walk across the centre in about fifteen minutes, but it has so much inside that you would need at least a year to explore it fully both above and below ground.

Walking along the Quayside now, it is difficult to ignore the revitalising spirit that has spread over the river to the Gateshead bank and the beckoning sights of the BALTIC and the Sage, especially when a

stroll over the Millennium Bridge is so inviting. I have dared to include them in this book although they are not in Newcastle as from both of these buildings there are splendid views of the city. That has always been the problem with this book in as much as the dilemma has been not what to put in, but what to leave out. Hopefully though it will encourage people to explore and get to know this wonderful city just that little bit better.

Opposite: The River Tyne / Right: The Discovery Museum

THE CASTLE

It would be unthinkable to write a book about Newcastle upon Tyne and not to mention the building that gave the city its name. Nothing now remains of the earth and timber 'new castle' built by Robert Curthose, the son of William the Conqueror, in 1080. The Castle was built in a strong position some 30 metres above the Tyne, where the ground fell steeply away. To the north and east, the gorge of the Lort Burn protected its flanks.

By about 1134, outside the Castle, a town had begun to grow up and it took its name from the stronghold. The most impressive remains today are those of the Keep, constructed as part of the rebuilding in stone of the Castle by Henry II, a work that took ten years and cost the huge sum of £1,144.

At the time of the Civil War, the Royalist Mayor of Newcastle, Sir John Marley, repaired the Keep in 1643 and during the siege a year later, the town held out for three months and the Keep for a further two days after the rest of the city had fallen to the Scottish army. For its stout defence Charles I is said to have conferred on the town the motto 'Fortiter Defendit Triumphans' to accompany the coat of arms.

The Castle fell into decay until Newcastle Corporation bought it in the first decade of the nineteenth century. They built new battlements and replaced the roof to keep out the elements. The corporation also put some cannons onto the battlements so that they could be fired during great occasions and festive periods. Unfortunately, this ended in tragedy in 1812, with a cartridge exploding and a gunner being blown over the parapet to meet an early demise during the Ascension Day festivities when the Mayor processed down the river in his State Barge.

The Castle's greatest enemy however, was not the invading armies that attacked its walls throughout the centuries but the march of progress in the form of the railway. The modern east coast line runs right across the Castle, separating the Keep from the Blackgate. Even though it stands isolated and alone, when walking round it today, it is hard not to be impressed by the sheer power of the Keep.

Opposite and right: The Castle Keep

9

THE BLACKGATE

Today the Blackgate looks almost sedately genteel with its early seventeenth century house nestling on the old medieval gateway that once gave entrance to the Castle Keep. The first known reference to it being called the Black Gate occurs in 1649 and the name is thought to have originated from Patrick Black, a Newcastle man of note, who lived in the seventeenth century.

Dating from 1247-50, the gateway was built in the reign of King Henry III and was originally approached across a drawbridge. The building is roughly oval in shape and its arched passageways and vaulted guard chambers, with three arrow slits at the base, are mostly original whilst the house above was largely rebuilt by Alexander Stevenson, who rented the building from King James I. The fourth floor with its steep tiled roof is a relatively modern addition. How tall the original gatehouse was is unknown, but it probably had three floors.

In the nineteenth century, the Gate was recorded as a place of squalor, with houses crushed together and stacked on top of each other. One writer described them as 'grotesque tenements' where the 'dense population, breathing into each others mouths' was worse than he had ever seen, even abroad.

We are lucky that we can still see this picturesque combination of architecture today, as it was nearly demolished in 1855 to make a roadway to the High Level Bridge. However, the public outcry was so great that, fortunately, the building was saved.

Below the outer half of the gate passage and visible beneath the modern bridge you can still see the slots in which the counterweights of the drawbridge swung. The wooden balustrade inside the arch also gives some idea of what it must have been like in here when the area was inhabited.

In 1851, around 103 people lived in eighteen households within the Blackgate and by 1855, the building was tenemented and used as shops and homes by second-hand shoe and clothes dealers, many from Scotland. There was even a much frequented public house inside called the Two Bulls' Heads.

Today we can see the entire entrance arch but this was not always so as buildings butted up to it and obscured about half of the frontage. These buildings were knocked down to create a road leading to the High Level Bridge.

Opposite: The Blackgate

The Blackgate, with St Nicholas' Cathedral and the city in the background.

THE ROMANS

Although there is little to see within the city boundaries of evidence of the Roman presence, their influence was immense. There are some fascinating remains in the Museum of Antiquities on the Newcastle University campus with inscribed stones and sculptures showing the names of military units and individuals that served here. There are also two matching altars from the Roman Bridge, dedicated to Neptune and Oceanus that were found in the riverbed when the Swing Bridge was being constructed. They were possibly put at the end of the bridge by the Sixth Legion to protect it from storms and floods.

The main indication of a Roman presence is the long straight thoroughfare of Westgate Road, which follows the line of Hadrian's Wall. The Wall continued across today's city passing through where the building of the Literary and Philosophical Society now stands, onwards to its final destination at the appropriately named Wallsend.

It is often forgotten that Hadrian's Wall was not just a defensive barrier on its own but part of a whole defensive system of forts, watch towers and beacons. One of these forts was built in a high defensive position above the Tyne and watched over the wall and the wooden bridge that crossed from the south bank in virtually the same place as the Swing Bridge does today.

The Roman's called the bridge Pons Aelius, the family name of the Emperor Hadrian being Aelius. It is estimated that the bridge was built around

The Roman Temple at Benwell

A.D. 122 and the fort, which took its name from the bridge, sometime later. Like other Roman bridges, it rested on stone piers and was constructed of a wooden platform probably being the same width as their roads. It says something for the Romans' skills as builders that both the Medieval and Georgian bridges used the Roman foundations for their own constructions.

The most tangible evidence to be seen is the remains of a small temple and a stone-built causeway that crossed the Vallum earthwork at Benwell, about 5 kilometres from the city centre.

HOLY JESUS HOSPITAL

The Holy Jesus Hospital was fortunate to survive the development plans of 1951 and 1963 and to avoid demolition, unlike its near neighbour the Royal Arcade.

Along with Alderman Fenwick's House, this almshouse is one of only two complete seventeenth century brick buildings still surviving in the city. The Keelmen's Hospital is also a brick built building but it was erected in 1701.

In many ways the Swan House, now 55⁰ North, roundabout has brought the building much more into the lives of Newcastle's residents, as to cross to Pilgrim Street from the east you walk alongside its thirty brick arches set on square pillars. Just outside the hospital entrance is a rather beautiful fountain. In the 1730's Bourne mentions in his 'History of Newcastle' the pleasant green field in front of the Hospital and the curious fountain which stands before the central doorway that was, on account of the new street in front, shifted from its original position which was further from the door.

In 1681, the Corporation of Newcastle founded the Holy Jesus Hospital, built on the site of an old Augustinian priory. In 1880, the Police Station, which adjoined the hospital on the west side, was replaced by a soup kitchen, built to blend in with the Hospital. The large 'Soup Kitchen' sign set into the stonework can still be seen today as you drive round the roundabout. Soup was sold between 8am and 12noon every working day for one penny a pint or eight pence a gallon. This is about 3.5p for four and a half litres of soup. The soup contained 'a pound of beef to every gallon with vegetables and proper seasoning in proportion'.

The building then entered a period of slow decline until in 1937 the hospital was declared 'unfit' and its resident staff of thirty-two sisters and eight brothers moved across the city to a new hospital at Spital Tongues, now a charitable trust that provides accommodation for the elderly poor of Newcastle.

The building remained empty for nearly forty years and its fabric suffered accordingly. In 1971, money from the John George Joicey Bequest allowed the building to be renovated and restored and it became the Joicey Museum.

The building is now owned by Newcastle City Council and leased to the National Trust who use it as the base for their Inner City Project. Information about the building and arrangements for visiting can be obtained from the National Trust.

Right: Holy Jesus Hospital

KEELMEN'S HOSPITAL

It would be unforgivable to produce a book on Newcastle without mentioning the coal trade and the wealth it generated for the city, contributing to what it is today. It is difficult to imagine just how important in the past the 'coals from Newcastle' were to the rest of the country. During the Civil War the Marquis of Newcastle, a Royalist, banned the selling of coal to the Parliamentary stronghold of London making the population vulnerable to starvation for want of coal for cooking fuel and for warmth. It is interesting to note that the wine merchants of Newcastle upon Tyne obtained port directly from Oporto in exchange for coal. Another example of a local business accepting goods in payment was when, in the early 1950s, a Newcastle book wholesaler, Harold Hill & Son Ltd. accepted oranges in payment for books exported to Israel.

Many people associate two well-known songs with Tyneside. Both of them, 'The Blaydon Races' and 'Fog on The Tyne' are instantly recognisable but there is a third much older and regarded by many of the city as being the original Geordie anthem and that is 'Weel May the Keel Row' which dates from around 1760. Keels were flat-bottomed boats that drew little water. The name comes from the weight of coal that they were able to carry, one keel equalling 21.5 tonnes. Characteristic of the keel was that it had a mast and a square sail, but if the wind dropped it could be propelled by using a long pole called a set, which had a forked iron prong at the end. The crews usually consisted of five men but the women would often pull keels along the river against the tide, before their load was discharged into sea-going colliers.

Keels are best described as looking like a wooden square bucket on a small boat and you can get a good idea from the sculpture in the Sandgate, a gate that was well used by the keelmen as an entry to the city. In 1701, the keelmen had raised some £2,000 to build a hospital for their use. The Hospital is one of the city's major landmarks and is remarkable in the fact that it was built and funded, not as the result of donations by the rich of the city, but by the keelmen themselves. Despite all this the keelmen were not allowed to run the Hospital and there were great disputes between them and the Company of Hostmen (coal owners) as to who should run the Hospital.

Gradually modern methods began to make the keelboats redundant and they finally passed away. It is amazing to realise in looking at the Keelmen's Hospital today that on the 10th June 1750, John Wesley preached to a congregation of thousands near here. The white tower, with its sundial clock and wind vane, now stands looking out over the Tyne as a fitting memorial to a group of men and women who have an important place in the city's history.

Right: The Keelmen's Hospital

THE PARISH CHURCH OF ST. JOHN THE BAPTIST

The Church of St. John the Baptist stands on the corner of Grainger Street and Westgate Road, its three storey, fifteenth century, tower can be seen from virtually the length of Grainger Street.

Like St. Andrew's, this Church has a superb font cover but this one is of a Restoration age and is a rich example of tabernacle work. The vaulting over the font incorporates the arms of Robert Rhodes, the wealthy merchant of the fifteenth century, who was benefactor to all the city's churches. He enlarged the fourteenth century south aisle to match that of the north and also paid for the south transept. The choir stalls were hand carved using an adze in 1935-6 by Robert Thompson from Yorkshire, who is well known for carving a mouse somewhere on everything he produced and St. John's is no exception, with four mice waiting to be discovered.

St. John's also contains the earliest known representation of the Arms of Newcastle upon Tyne in a window in the north wall and above it a roundel of surviving medieval glass from about 1400. Visible in the church is an opening in the form of a Greek cross, which was part of the wall of the cell of an anchorite, a man who had withdrawn from the world for religious reasons, from which he could watch the service.

Apart from the pews, the heating and the lighting, St. John's has changed little in its appearance since the mid-sixteenth century.

Buried in the churchyard is Edward Chicken, author of 'The Collier's Wedding', a local poem, famous in the nineteenth century, containing much rough humour and local colour. In 1829, John Dobson restored the chancel and the gables and you will find a tablet honouring Richard Grainger on the south wall of the interior next to the door.

During the plague in Newcastle in October 1567, 128 people from St. John's Parish died .

A ghost is supposed to frequent the tower stairs. Despite an exorcism in the 1970's the spectre hasn't moved out. Now and again the person ringing the sixth bell, which is nearest the stairs, will turn to see who is coming up.

The Parish Church of St John the Baptist

NORMANS

After the Romans left Newcastle, the area within the walls of their fort was colonised first by the Romano-British people of the area and then the Saxons, and slowly but surely the small settlement of Monkchester began to take shape.

In 1080 Robert Curthose, son of William the Conqueror, halted his army at Monkchester and on the King's orders built a new castle where the present keep now stands. This was probably a wooden structure and was put up very quickly, under its shelter, Monkchester prospered and in 1091, the first church on the site of St. Nicholas' Cathedral was built.

In 1095, Robert Mowbray, Earl of Northumberland, instigated a revolt against William Rufus, who had succeeded to the throne after the Conqueror's death. Thoroughly defeating Mowbray and imprisoning him for life for good measure, William realised that he needed a much stronger power base here, so he replaced the wooden castle with one of stone, repaired the Roman walls where needed and built new walls to allow Monkchester to grow. He also repaired the bridge over the Tyne and built many new houses.

During the reign of King Stephen, the Earldom of Northumberland passed into Scottish hands, so not being threatened by the Scots, the town of New Castle as it had become known, prospered with monastic settlements, streets and markets being set up outside the walls. Under the Normans, the town grew steadily and the origins of many of the streets we know today, such as Pilgrim Street and Newgate Street, sprang up.

Henry II regained the Earldom of Northumberland for the English crown soon after and in 1168 started building the keep as seen today. The keep is the most visible evidence of the Norman presence in the city, but there are others. Amongst these is St. Andrew's Church in Newgate Street, said to date from the middle of the twelfth century with one of its outstanding features being its Norman chancel arch.

The Normans may not have left a great deal to see from their presence in the city but their influence has been immense; if nothing else, were it not for them the city would probably be called Monkchester instead of Newcastle upon Tyne.

Right: The City Walls near Stowell Street

THE QUAYSIDE

F ew places epitomise the vibrant resurgence of Newcastle more than the Quayside. Not only is it renowned for its cafés, bars and restaurants and superb examples of stunning modern architecture but it also has become something of an external art gallery in its own right.

Some of the highlights of these pieces of art, all from 1996, include the relief sculpture, by Neil Talbot, sited near the Wesley Memorial, of one hundred carvings on a sandstone wall depicting well-known sights along the Tyne and Andre Wallace's 8.7 metres high steel column topped with a bronze statue of a mythical river god. To many though it is the Blacksmith's Needle, by the Members of the British Association of Blacksmiths Artists, that catches the eye, this 7.6 metres high steel sculpture has a maritime theme represented by bells, mermaids, shells and various sea creatures. Close by is the 1998 Swirle Pavilion by Raf Fulcher, both a sculpture and a building. The names of the towns carved around it are taken from a faded sign of a local shipping company found in nearby Plummer Chare that showed its destinations. The name Swirle refers to the stream, which flows into the Tyne underneath the promenade at this point.

Originally the Quayside began at the Tyne Bridge, ran for about 500 metres towards the Sandgate, and then continued as the New Quay. Since the middle ages the buildings of the Quayside have been separated by narrow alleys or chares with names such as Peppercorn Chare and Blue Anchor Chare that lead up to the city.

Above: Blacksmith's Needle and Quayside / Below left: Swirle Pavilion / Below right: Copthorne Hotel

In 1854, a fire broke out in a worsted factory in Gateshead and spread to a warehouse containing 3,000 tonnes of sulphur, 130 tonnes of saltpetre, 5 tonnes of turpentine and naphtha. The resulting explosion killed 53 people most of whom had come to watch the fire from the Quayside. Burning timbers were thrown across the Tyne setting fire to the old medieval buildings on the Newcastle Quayside causing great destruction for a length of over 100 metres.

Since the 1980s an era of regeneration has been happening on the Newcastle Quayside. The shift in business away from the banks of the Tyne caused by the Central Station and Grainger's redevelopment meant that much of the Quayside was ripe for development and property on the waterside became fashionable again. Each Sunday morning the area from the Tyne Bridge eastwards is a hive of activity as the Quayside Market takes place until mid-afternoon. The stalls here sell just about everything, with quite a few bargains on offer if you know where to look. When the shopping fever has died down many visitors retire to the Quayside pubs or restaurants.

One thing that has never changed is the desire of the population to enjoy life. Though still having a serious rival in the Bigg Market there is no doubt that the Newcastle Quayside has become one of the places for a night out and to live, especially in the many attractive and desirable apartments and penthouses over-looking the river.

Residential development, East Quayside

Sunday Market, Quayside / Opposite: Blacksmith's Needle, Quayside

SANDHILL

It must have been one of the sights of England to come off the Medieval Tyne Bridge with its shops and houses, in the seventeenth century, and see the open triangle of land at Sandhill with the great timber framed houses that still stand today.

At that time, they would have been majestic, freshly painted with shops on the ground floor and the wealthy merchants' rooms and offices above. Sandhill was the very heart of the town, where justice was handed out, government carried on, and where at Midsummer and on St. Peter's Eve, great bonfires were lit by the Company of Cooks.

At the end of the bridge, on entering Sandhill, stood the Chapel and Hospital of St. Thomas the Martyr. They were finally demolished in 1830 and the present Watergate Building designed by John Dobson was put up in their place.

No longer is there a hill at Sandhill but just the flat, level space on which the Town Hall was sited, just to the east of The Watergate. The Town Hall stood for 250 years and during that time the Mayor's and Sheriff's Courts, The Admiralty or River Court, Guild meetings and the Court of Pyepowder were held here. In 1665, the Town Hall was demolished and the present Guildhall was built.

This was one of the most bustling areas of the old city, with its markets and children playing in the waters of the Lort Burn and on the sands of the river. Many packhorses stood waiting patiently to carry goods up the Side to the houses above and the air would have been thick with the cries of traders and

Sandhill

street vendors.

Of the seven old houses remaining in Sandhill, five of them are in one section called the Red House. Number 32 is the original Red House, directly opposite the Guildhall and in its time has been a tea and coffee warehouse.

The Court of Pyepowder derived its name from the French 'pied poundre' or poor foot, as this was the court that people with no money could apply to for justice.

BESSIE SURTEES' HOUSE

Sandhill was the centre of the medieval town and the houses remaining here are prime examples of the type of architecture you would find in any prosperous city centre of the time. Of all these buildings Bessie Surtees' house is probably the best known. This was once two houses, which were amalgamated in the twentieth century. These houses became known by the surnames of the merchant families who lived in them in the seventeenth century, Millbank and Surtees.

The steeple on top of St. Nicholas Cathedral was given to the church by Robert Rhodes, a wealthy merchant, who lived in the house in 1465. To most people it is the romantic story of elopement that will be forever associated with the house.

Bessie was the daughter of Aubone Surtees a prominent, wealthy banker in the city, in the late eighteenth century. She was described as a great beauty who fell in love with John Scott, the son of a coal-fitter from nearby Love Lane. As her father did not approve of the match, the two met in secret until on the 18th of November 1772 they eloped and crossed into Scotland to be married. A blue pane now marks the window used by Bessie to elope.

It was not long before both fathers forgave them and John started to read law. He became very successful and in 1783 entered Parliament. He became Solicitor-General, was knighted and in 1793 became Attorney-General, in 1799 Lord Chief Justice of the Common Pleas and then eventually in 1801 he rose to the office of Lord Chancellor.

English Heritage took over the house in 1989 and they have done a magnificent job in opening up the ground floor of the house to the public. The free entry to the house enables us to get an idea of the opulence enjoyed by the city's successful merchants. The first floor room is the largest in the house and has oak panelling with a magnificent ceiling. It is easy to imagine the merchant looking out over the quayside from this room, sipping from his glass of malmsey wine as his ships were unloaded.

Bessie Surtees' House

SIDE

Side is one of the city's oldest streets, one being the only main thoroughfare that connected the town on the higher ground with the quayside below. This state of affairs lasted until the construction of Dean Street in the 1780s.

Side was split into three distinct streets known as Side, Cordwainer's Row and Flesher Row. One of the city's most famous sons, Admiral Lord Collingwood, was born here in 1748 in a house on a site now occupied by Milburn House built in 1902. Milburn House was home to shipping companies such as Cunard, White Star and P&O; indeed the floor levels were lettered rather than numbered as with the decks on a ship.

Today the street is still a delight, from the traditional gentlemen's barber with its red and white pole at the top, to the steep Dogleap Stairs leading up to the Castle. It is hard to imagine what it must have been like to live in the crowded tenements that bordered either side in the nineteenth century.

Indeed photographs of Side taken in 1863 show timber framed houses on opposite sides of the street, overhanging the road and practically touching in the middle. The gloominess of the street, as very little light could enter it, was much commented upon by early writers and it must have been very difficult to move goods up it in the depths of winter with snow and ice on its cobbled surface. At this time too, Side was still used by people to avoid paying the tolls on the High Level Bridge and was noted for having many bookmakers along its length.

The wide railway viaduct that crosses high above was built in 1849, then widened in 1893, a fact that can be seen by the different coloured brick work in the next section, on the north side.

The street today has a variety of shops, but one of the most well known is the Side Photographic Gallery which has a national reputation for showing the very best work. At the bottom of the street, on the west side, can be seen a marvellous old courtyard with stairs climbing up into, what once must have been, a warren of houses and dwellings.

At its base Side merged into Sandhill and Butcher Bank, so called because of all the butchers who traded or lived there, as it was close to the Flesh Market. Today it is called Akenside Hill after the Newcastle physician and poet Mark Akenside. He was born at number 33 and received his education at the Royal Free Grammar School, was later a pupil at Wilson's Academy and rose to the position of physician to the Queen in 1761.

PANDONGATE HOUSE

Pandongate House is a former Victorian bonded warehouse located on the corner of City Road that epitomizes the regeneration of redundant buildings and a return to people living in the city centre areas. Like many quayside developments in Newcastle it is popular with working professionals who are in the wonderful position of being able to enjoy both the relaxing views of the river flowing by and the buzz of the quayside bars and restaurants.

Above: Dean Street / Pandongate House

CLOSE

Before the coming of the Swing Bridge only small vessels could pass above Sandhill so there was no need for large wharves and a quayside. As a result, houses were built up either side of the roadway instead of just on the side facing the river. Sandwiched between the cliff of the Tyne gorge and the riverbank the houses were very close together and the area and the road became known as Close.

At the western end of the street was Close Gate with the Riverside Tower that formed the southernmost limit of the city walls, for a time it was the meeting place of the Sailmakers' Company, but now no trace of it remains. Close Gate was used as a prison and as a meeting place for the House Carpenters' Company but it was demolished in 1797 mainly because its entrance was so narrow.

The riverside is now lined with plush new hotels when not that long ago Close was a quiet narrow street where the gentry and nobility of Newcastle had their homes, amongst these were Sir John Marley and Sir William Blackett. Some of the houses in this stretch were magnificent but the only one remaining is the Cooperage below the piers of the High Level Bridge. This is one of the oldest houses in the city and was for many years the coopering business of the Arthur family.

There is little left of the huge warehouses that once stood here, but the remains of the steep paths with such names as Breakneck Stairs that lead up to the city are still visible. At the foot of Tuthill Stairs was the Mansion House, which was the official residence of the Mayor. The gilded State Barge of the Mayor was kept here for Barge Day when it joined the barges of Trinity House and the various trades companies to progress down to the river's mouth to proclaim the jurisdiction of the city over the river. It must have been an amazing sight with everyone in fine costumes and a flotilla of bedecked boats.

While preparing for Barge Day in May 1837 the workmen were trying out some new guns, when sadly Andrew Percy was killed as one of the guns exploded when he was striking the ramrod with a hammer.

The Cooperage, Close

CHARES & STAIRS

Some idea of the old town, before the classical streets of Grainger Town were built, can be discovered by exploring the chares and lonnens, which still survive either side of the Groat and Cloth Markets.

High Bridge, for example, connecting the Bigg Market with Grey Street, is an attractive street but in terms of width, it is virtually a motorway in medieval terms as most of the lanes then were less than a metre wide. Another example is to look at White Hart Yard, still with its cobbles and wheel worn granite gutters and overhead lifting gantries, and Old George Yard further along. Pudding Chare runs from the Bigg Market to Westgate Road and is said to be named after the Pow Dene, a small river that runs under the pavement, which was bridged and eventually buried. It flowed into the Tyne underneath Burn Bank Chare a narrow, crooked alleyway that runs nearly above it.

Some have been forgotten or renamed. Leazes Lane, for example, was known as Myln Chare as it lead up to Chimney Mills. Another name for it was Blindman's Alley which it got from a blind man who used it to beg a penny from passersby.

Manor Chare and Broad Chare still carry commerce today as they did in the great days of the quayside. Trinity House, one of the great treasure chests of the city's history was situated in Broad Chare. Most Newcastle people associate the chares with the Quayside area and their ascending steep slopes to the city. Beside the new law courts is Cox Chare, once called Coxton's Chare.

Walking eastwards you come to Love Lane, which in the seventeenth century was known as 'Gowerly's Rawe' and was famous as the birthplace of the two Scott brothers, William Scott, Lord Stowell (Stowell Street) and John Scott, Lord Eldon, (Eldon Square) who eloped with Bessie Surtees.

Walking down Forth Banks you enter Close, where Close Gate once stood. Here, by the huge Spoors Warehouse, you can see two stairs winding their way up. Eventually you will come to Breakneck Stairs hugging the side of Hanover Gardens.

Modern steps take you up to Hanover Street where a stone tramway still remains in the road, the smooth slabs being for the wagon wheels and the cobbles to give the horses grip as they toiled up the steep slope.

Further along are Tuthill Stairs and just as you enter Sandhill, before passing under the High Level Bridge, is Long Stairs. Standing at the bottom and looking up it's easy to see how it got its name. On the other side of the bridge is Castle Stairs that lead up by a series of right-angled turns to Castle Garth. Up here, Dogleap Stairs leads from just past Blackgate down into Side.

Above: Baltic Chambers, Quayside Left: Hanover Street

 Around 1827 or so, according to Mackenzie in his history of Newcastle upon Tyne, Plummer Chare was known as the receptacle of Cyprian Nymphs, whose blandishments were of the most coarse and vulgar nature.

TRINITY HOUSE

Trinity House, Quayside

There are many 'time capsules' in Newcastle still carrying out their original purpose but the most impressive has to be Trinity House. It must also lay a claim to be one of the most interesting buildings in the city. Tucked away in Broad Chare, although it can also be approached from Trinity Chare, it could be passed without notice.

Walk through its doorway and the Tudor origins jump out especially on entering the first courtyard, with an anchor from a ship of the Spanish Armada mounted on the wall. This is no museum but a working maritime organisation, dedicated to safe navigation and welfare of seamen with its Master continuing the long line of holders of that post since the days of the Tudors.

The Guild of Fraternity of the Blessed Trinity of Newcastle upon Tyne was established in 1505, the organisation was granted a Royal Charter of Incorporation in 1536 by King Henry VIII and it has operated by Royal Charter ever since.

Most of the old city guilds have ceased to exist but the brethren of Trinity House continue to play a vital part in the life of the city by carrying out the examination and licensing of deep-sea pilots. Besides this, Trinity House administers education and training programmes for youth organisations such as the sea cadets and sea scouts.

From its birth, Trinity House was a religious institution, to train seaman and maintain a guild in honour of the Trinity. On entering the Great Hall and vestibule there is an awareness of entering not only another time but also another world, one of a distinct nautical nature.

The chapel, completed in 1634, has a wonderful series of box pews with arches and angels' heads on their doors. Other treasures include the Master's room with its mahogany table and bookshelves lining one wall, here a secret door, leading to the chapel, is hidden by shelves of dummy books. The sumptuousness of the Banqueting Hall is awesome with its huge maritime paintings and gilded ceiling.

As well as the marvellous maritime paintings and models of ships, the rooms contain many hundreds of fascinating artefacts gathered by Tyne seafarers from the four corners of the globe, including sea creatures, jewellery, paintings and weapons.

Even outside the buildings and courtyards are impressive as they unfold and open up around you as they are explored. The main courtyard, which once housed the pensioners of the Brethren, has on its north side, a building with three storeys, but when walking down Dog Bank behind, it seems to have only a single storey.

This is possibly the oldest building in Newcastle as it may well be a twelfth century townhouse. The buildings all have crests above them naming the Master at the time of their construction; most are almshouses but there is also a school showing that Trinity House always has, and continues to play a part in the education of the city's youth.

To look round Trinity House you really need to book a tour.

 On 28th August 1838, the Master and Brethren of Trinity House presented the Freedom of Newcastle, in silver boxes, to Captain Sir George Back and Captain J.C. Cross, R.N. for their help to the crews of the whaling ships frozen in the ice during the winter of 1837.

SANDGATE

Sandgate allowed traffic to pass through the town walls on the eastern side of Newcastle. It gave its name to a much larger settlement outside the walls, first recorded in 1485, which became the area where most of the keelmen lived dominating the eastern parishes of All Saints' and St. Ann's. Considering the enormous part they played in the city's development, it is odd that the only memorial to them is the Keelmen's Hospital on City Road.

At the point where Sandgate met the Milk Market, although meat could also be bought here, stood the Sandgate Pant where every Saturday an old clothes fair was held. It was also known as Paddy's Market due to the large number of Irish immigrants who settled here.

This area was the most densely populated part of the town and the tenements and lodging houses of Sandgate were appallingly cramped and overcrowded with virtually no sanitation. Often the main source of water was from the Tyne, a factor that contributed to the cholera epidemics that occasionally ravaged the area.

During the siege of 1644, the area was so densely packed with houses along the narrow chares that the suburb was set alight by the defenders so it would not give cover to the Scots. A fort was built outside the walls during the siege and later it became the dumping ground for waste and rubbish and became known as Sandgate Midden with the contents being sold for manure. The gate itself was demolished in 1798 with part of the adjoining city wall.

The Malmaison Hotel, Quayside

The Swirle Pavilion / Opposite: The Law Courts, Quayside

Henry Bourne described it in 1736 as 'a vast number of narrow lanes...crowded with houses'. Indeed nineteenth century photographs of such places as Addy's Entry and Sellar's Entry show dark narrow alleyways with open sewers running down the sides of buildings.

The road running through the middle of Sandgate had an unenviable reputation amongst the more genteel citizens of the town and was considered quite a dangerous place after dark. Sandgate still runs up the hill but today the area could hardly be more different. In stark contrast to the dreadful living conditions of the past, the Sandgate is now a fine example of the blending of new buildings with old refurbished warehouses containing modern apartments. Another illustration of a new use for an old building is the North Eastern Co-operative warehouse, which has been converted into the Malmaison Hotel and the top of the façade stills bears testimony to the Co-op.

CIVIL WAR

From its earliest days, Newcastle's history has always had a strong connection with the business of war. Over the centuries, many citizens rallied to the colours of various regiments and causes.

On occasion, the city has had to defend itself behind its walls, with the most momentous of these sieges commencing in August 1644, when a Scottish army, loyal to the parliamentary cause, surrounded the town.

The Mayor, Sir John Marley, proved himself 'no carpet knight from a tap house' and set about strengthening the defences of the town. He started by deepening the ditch around the walls so that any scaling-ladders used by the besiegers would be too short. Stone and lime were used to cement in the embrasures of the battlements with a sniping slit installed for sharpshooters to operate from, very similar to the crossbow slits of a few centuries earlier. Great guns were placed on the round tower at the south end of where the Moot Hall stands to counterbalance the five gun batteries placed by the Scottish army on the south bank of the Tyne.

A Parliamentary battery in the Sandgate beat down the upper part of what is known today as the Sally Port or Carpenters' Tower. Later the northwest wall near St. Andrew's Church was blasted to within less than a metre from the ground but the defenders immediately barricaded it with timber and anything else they could find. Although the church suffered considerably, the same cannot be said of the beautiful spire of St. Nicholas' Church, although this might

be because the Scots were aware that prisoners were deliberately held under the lantern!

On October 19th, four huge breaches were made in the section of the wall still standing behind Orchard Street by mines laid underneath it. You can still see where they were repaired afterwards, but the slopes of the rubble were very steep and difficult to clamber up and this resulted in an horrific slaughter.

Walk down Close today by the corner of Forth Banks and it is difficult to imagine that when the Buccleugh regiments poured into the town, through a breach in the walls above Close Gate, that Marley's cavalry carried out three charges to try to disperse them. They were unsuccessful and at Pilgrim Gate with its barbican, roughly where the top of Pilgrim Street is today, Captain George Errington and 180 town tradesmen were attacked from the rear by troops coming up through the town and were forced to surrender. The Bigg Market, then much larger than today, was soon filled with the defenders from the wall, laying down their arms.

As a result of the town falling into Parliamentarien hands, King Charles I was brought here and imprisoned in Anderson Place. In an attempt to escape along the Lort Burn, which in later years was covered over to became Grey Street and Dean Street, he got as far as a grate in Side. As a result of this attempt, he was stopped from practising golf on the Shieldfield and was now watched more closely by his guards who annoyed him immensely by smoking.

The City Walls near Stowell Street

King Charles' coachman, Hugh Brown, died while in the King's Service in Newcastle and was buried on the 6th December 1646, in St. Andrew's Churchyard, as noted by Sykes in his 'Local Records'.

THE RIVER TYNE

Since Roman times the people of Newcastle have used the river to import and export a variety of commodities. For example, in the early fourteenth century the wealth of the city was principally derived from the export of hides, wool and coal despite the fact that wool from sheep north of the Tees was considered poor quality.

In the seventeenth century, merchants imported timber for pit props, pitch, hemp, flax and traded coal in exchange. It is interesting to note that by the mid seventeenth century London had become completely dependent on shipments of coal from Newcastle.

A milestone in the history of the Tyne came in the next century with the passing in 1850 of the River Tyne Improvement Act by which Gateshead, Tynemouth, South Shields, and the Admiralty all had to share, with Newcastle, responsibility for the River Tyne. The first move of the new Commission was to obtain permission to build two substantial piers at the river entrance to enable shipping to navigate the mouth in safety. This, connected with the development and invention of steamships, railways, furnaces and the tapping of deeper coal seams with the almost simultaneous foundation of two of Newcastle's heavyweight companies Armstrong's and Palmer's, set the scene for a period of rapid industrial expansion along the banks of the river.

Natural forces have also played a part in the history of the river, which has not always been benevolent. The Great Flood of 1771 brought huge damage to the Sandhill area, sweeping away parts of the old Tyne Bridge and just over a hundred years later disaster struck again when ice carried away scaffolding being used for the construction of the Redheugh Bridge.

There have been times when ice has brought benefits to the citizens of Newcastle as when it was so cold that the river froze over to a considerable depth and it was possible to hold Frost Fairs. In 1739, tents were set up and markets and entertainment lasted for some six

Sunset on the Tyne

weeks. There are reports that skating races were held on the frozen Tyne for up to four miles below the bridge. Bonfires were lit on the ice when the river froze in 1814 and hundreds of people walked and skated across the river.

In the early half of the nineteenth century, traffic on the Tyne increased to a level that saw hundreds of boats ferrying goods to and from ships and factories. This produced a breed of men who became expert in the use of the oar. Thousands would come to the river to watch rowing races, especially when the Thames Watermen issued a challenge, which in turn led to the rise of the regions first sporting superstars. Great amounts of money were waged on the professional races held on the river and as a result, amateur clubs sprang up along the banks. Others too had not been slow to see the recreational possibilities of the water and the Newcastle Motor Boat Club was formed in the 1920s and still sails today from the mouth of the Ouseburn.

Although in the past the river had provided a bountiful harvest of salmon that swim up it each year to spawn, the explosive expansion of industry and the increase in the city's population brought with it considerable pollution. In recent years, the Environment Agency has achieved great success in cleaning up the Tyne and as the water quality continues to improve, the salmon and sea trout numbers are increasing again. Over 200,000 fish have been recorded migrating upriver since 1996.

On December 2nd 1839, a fine specimen of meagre, a large Mediterranean fish, one of the largest of scaly fishes, was caught in the Tyne. It measured 5 feet 2 inches and was purchased by the Natural History Society.

In 1559, Alderman Anderson was leaning over the Tyne Bridge when his signet ring fell into the water. His servant bought a salmon later and on opening it, the ring was found inside!

Left: Bridges of the Tyne / Right: Tall Ships, Quayside

THE TYNE BRIDGES

In the summer of 1872, the work of dismantling the old Georgian bridge across the Tyne to prepare for the construction of the Swing Bridge was well under way. On removing the third pier from the Gateshead side, it was discovered that the foundations of all three bridges could be seen.

The Medieval builders had used the Roman foundations and the Georgians had used both in the fabric of their own bridge. What is particularly interesting to us today is that the Victorian superintendent thought that the Roman carpentry was superior to the two others.

This continuing story of bridge building shows that for nearly two thousand years people have crossed the Tyne at this point. The bridge has not always been the width we see at present as the Roman structure was kept to 5.5 metres which was the standard width of their military roads, whilst the Medieval structure was far wider than the Georgian bridge as this helped to strengthen it against the water of the river. So wide it was that it had towers, shops, houses and a chapel built upon its twelve arches; three of these arches were filled in and used for storage space when the quays on both banks were built.

In November 1771, the Tyne flooded, drowning Sandhill and the Quayside almost down to the Ouseburn. The pressure of water was so great that the arches and houses collapsed into the river. The Georgian bridge was built of stone and had parapets along its length but stopped the bigger vessels passing up the Tyne, so with the technological developments going on upstream at Elswick, its demise was only a matter of time.

The other bridges across the river have their own story to tell and some are not restricted to carrying only road, rail and foot traffic. The Redheugh Bridge carries a water main and two gas mains that were originally carried by the previous structure as well as electricity and telephone cables. Small portholes are installed in the fabric to ventilate the channels and prevent the concentration of gas and

Opposite: The Gateshead Millennium Bridge / Right: The Tyne Bridge

potential leaks that might create an explosion. The Redheugh Bridge also has a double set of waterproofing under its roadways to prevent the salt, used for clearing the ice and snow during the winter, from filtering through and attacking the steel reinforcements in the concrete.

People piled onto the High Level Bridge to watch the Great Fire of 1854 that ignited buildings on both banks. It also attracted one Stephen Jeffrey known as 'Jeffrey the Diver' who would jump off bridges then pass the hat around. While attempting this in 1865 he was caught by the police and prevented from doing so. However, in his place a stranger from Hartlepool made the jump and took his own hat round instead! The bridge also came close to being burned down in 1866 when the flames from a fire nearby ignited the asphalt timber decking.

It must be said that the bridges have played an important part in the city's development and will no doubt continue to do so as long as the water flows beneath them.

On 10th May 1856, some workmen were demolishing the premises of Mr. Dickinson, the tobacconist, at the Head of Side, to make way for an approach to the High Level Bridge. Remains of an ancient building, which originally stood on the site were unearthed. A fourteenth century doorway with two windows was laid bare as well as an oaken roof of a large apartment. The building had apparently undergone extensive alterations after the Reformation as portions of the windows were in Tudor style. Although no records of the building were discovered, it was probably of a monastic character. Two very large antlers were also found nearby about sixteen feet below the surface.

Five generations of royalty have opened River Tyne crossings:
Queen Victoria opened the High Level Bridge in 1849.
King Edward VII opened the King Edward VII Bridge in 1906.
King George V opened the Tyne Bridge in 1928.
Queen Elizabeth II opened the Tyne Tunnel in 1981, the Queen Elizabeth II Bridge in 1981, the Blaydon Bridge in 1990, and the Gateshead Millennium Bridge in 2002.
Diana, Princess of Wales opened the Redheugh Bridge in 1983.

Looking across the Tyne Bridge to the city

THE SWING BRIDGE

A Sunday stroll over the Tyne bridges has become quite popular in recent years and the present Swing Bridge is the latest in a line to cross the Tyne at this point. The Romans built the first bridge on this spot as part of the defensive system of Hadrian's Wall. To them the wooden bridge built on stone piers was known as the Pons Aelius and was probably finished around A.D.120.

During the Middle Ages the bridge was rebuilt entirely in stone and furnished with a row of houses and a chapel, unfortunately this structure was swept away by the great Tyne flood of 1771. A replacement was soon installed and pictures of it bring to mind Berwick's present old stone bridge. A century later, it too was replaced as the low arches prohibited river traffic passing upstream to Armstrong's factory at Elswick. It also stopped large shipments of coal being brought downriver so this had to be done by the keelboats, which was uneconomic.

The present bridge was built in its place and construction took no less than eight years, finally being opened in June 1876. The Swing Bridge's design enabled deep-sea craft to use the river that had been recently dredged, and warships built at Armstrong's factories in Elswick were now able to reach the open sea.

A temporary bridge was erected in 1865-1866 so that the old bridge could be dismantled and machinery for the new one installed. It is interesting to note, and probably entirely logical, that Armstrong's mechanism on which the bridge swings is based on a system of rollers resembling the mechanism of a gun turret.

Armstrong built the new cantilevered bridge, driven by steam pumps and weighing over 1,200 tonnes. The hydraulic machinery pivoted the bridge at right angles to lie parallel with the banks and so allow ships upstream. These pumps lasted until 1959 when electric pumps finally replaced them. However, most of the original design features are still in working order and in use today.

The Swing Bridge, with the Castle and St Nicholas' Cathedral in the background

Above and opposite: The Swing Bridge

THE GUILDHALL

Newcastle had a Guildhall in the thirteenth century and although nothing is known of this early hall, in all probability, it stood in Sandhill on the same site as the present Guildhall. When in 1412 Roger Thornton founded his hospital or almshouse for the poor and the sick, he mentioned it was established in a house he had built in Sandhill on the east side of the Guildhall.

By the time of the Restoration Newcastle upon Tyne appeared to have made a full recovery from all loss and damage from the Civil War. Perhaps the clearest indication of this was the construction of the Guildhall and Exchange in Sandhill.

In 1655, the old hall was enlarged by taking in land to the west and by incorporating Thornton's Hospital, also known as the 'Maison Dieu'. The new building erected between 1655 and 1658 was designed by Robert Trollope of York in a peculiar combination of Renaissance and Gothic styles with doors connecting both buildings and a common staircase giving access to the new Town Court and 'Maison Dieu'.

The municipal and assize courts of session were held here and the building housed the offices of the corporation. During the eighteenth century the Guildhall twice suffered serious damage, once in 1740 by Keelmen rioting in protest at the scarcity and price of corn and again in 1791 when it was damaged by fire.

The steps of the Guildhall were a favourite preaching spot of John Wesley, the Methodist minister.

Once, when threatened by some rough elements in the crowd, he was saved by Mrs. Bailes, a fishwife, who threw one arm around his waist and with the other raised her fist in defiance of the mob daring anyone to come near them.

In 1796, the Common Council decided to take the opportunity to reconstruct and modernise the entire north front. The new front was set further back and was built in the same rather severe, classical style as the Assembly Rooms and Moot Hall. Further radical alterations took place in 1823 when John Dobson redesigned the building and made alterations to the east end where on the upper level, large doors lead into the Merchant's Court with its fine panelled wainscoting reaching almost to the ceiling. A huge carved oak chimneypiece takes up most of the space on the east wall.

These alterations also included a colonnaded fish market and Margaret Jane Dobson in her 'Memoir' (1885) says 'Mr Dobson designed the fish market, Sandhill, Newcastle, the business of which was previously carried out in the open air. The good ladies who presided over the stalls seriously objected to being removed from their old quarters and for some time Mr Dobson received such an impolite reception from them that he was obliged to avoid their presence.

But when bad weather came and they realised the comfort of their new abode, they relented, and a deputation of fair dames arrived at his residence in Newbridge Street with a peace offering of fish for a

Christmas dinner. Ever after that he was their 'cannie Mr Dobson.' (Mackenzie 1827).

The last major change to the building occurred in 1880 when the open colonnaded fish market, which stood below the new Merchant Adventurer's Court, was walled up giving the building its present day appearance.

Over the last decade, significant public funds and private sector resources have been invested in the regeneration of the Newcastle and Gateshead Quaysides. The area has been transformed into a destination for businesses, visitors and local people. As part of this transformation the Guildhall, a Grade 1 listed building, has now had an extensive internal refurbishment. The revitalised Guildhall will house the new Tourist Information Centre, which is designed to meet all the information needs of the ever increasing number of visitors to the area. It has also created a fantastic opportunity to open the Guildhall, a prestigious heritage asset, to the public.

The Guildhall

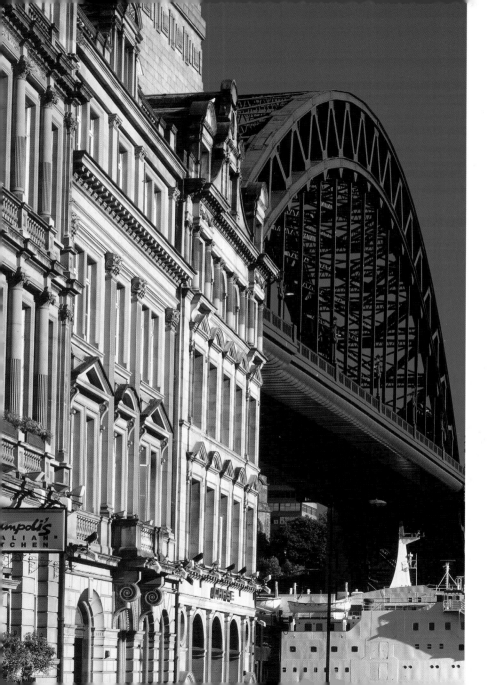

THE TYNE BRIDGE

There are many buildings in the city of Newcastle upon Tyne that are not as their architect fully expected them to look, the portico at the Central Station being a good example.

This is certainly also true of the Tyne Bridge as it was originally intended to have massive triumphal arches at each end. Opened by King George V in 1928, the Tyne Bridge was once the world's largest single span bridge, with the exception of the Sydney Harbour Bridge. Like its Australian cousin, the Tyne Bridge was built out progressively from both banks. In fact, a Middlesbrough company won the contracts for both in 1928, and the designer of the Sydney Harbour Bridge was also the consulting engineer on the Tyne Bridge.

There is some debate as to which of the two bridges was built first. Work on the Sydney Bridge was started before the Tyne Bridge, but because the Sydney Bridge is much larger and more complicated in its travel carriage-ways, the Tyne Bridge was finished first, three years before the completion of the Australian bridge.

The road on the Tyne Bridge can claim to be one of the shortest numbered roads in the country as approached from the south and north it is numbered the A167 and the A167 (M) respectively, however once on the bridge it becomes the A6127. The roadway is suspended from a graceful and gigantic arch, reaching a height of some 37 metres above the high tide mark with the foundations set some 25 metres below it. On each bank, the road passes through two great piers made of Cornish granite, designed by the Newcastle architect Robert Burns Dick. They were originally planned to be five storied warehouses and one of them contained a lift to carry pedestrians and goods up from the quayside, but this is no longer in use. The bridge is used by approximately 60,000 vehicles a day and major deterioration of the 1928 road and walkways resulted in serious renovation in 1999. The fragility of the metal plates of the walkway meant that a weight limit had to be put upon the work so that much of it was done by hand, almost recreating the 1928 methods.

Left: The Tyne Bridge

The bridge has become the most famous of all the city's buildings and is still the most iconic, despite the arrival of the new Gateshead Millennium Bridge. It will be forever associated with the swarming mass of runners crossing it as part of the Great North Run and the incredible fireworks display set off from it at the dawn of the twenty-first century.

The total length, including approaches, is 389 metres.

The total height, above the high water level, is 59 metres.

The length of the main arch span, pier to pier, is 162 metres.

The bridge is 7 metres wide while the approaches are 24 metres wide.

The weight of the steelwork in the arch alone is 3,556 tonnes.

The total weight of the steelwork, including approaches, is 7,112 tonnes.

Tramlines were laid on the bridge on its construction and the last tram crossed the bridge on the 5th March 1950.

The bridge not only spans the river but also has a political function. The Tyne Bridge constituency includes the Newcastle Benwell, Elswick, Scotswood and West City wards and on the south of the river covers the Gateshead wards of Bede, Bensham, Deckham, Dunstan, Saltwell and Teams.

When first mooted in 1883 the construction costs of the bridge were estimated to be around £200,000, which was to be divided one-third to Gateshead and two-thirds to Newcastle.

The Tyne Bridge was once said to carry more traffic than the Severn, Forth and Humber road bridges combined.

If you are reading this book in some far flung corner of the world and are feeling homesick, you can log on to web-cam sites that show the bridge and its traffic flow.

Right: The Tyne Bridge

The Tyne Bridge at night

Bridges across the Tyne

Competitors in the Great North Run cross the Tyne Bridge

The River Tyne and bridges

THE HIGH LEVEL BRIDGE

The High Level Bridge is one of the most important structures in the history of the British railway system. Robert Stephenson's bridge completed the last section of the London to Edinburgh rail link and confirmed the east coast line as the major route between the two cities. Before its completion, it was necessary to get off the train at Newcastle's Central Station and either walk or take a cab to Gateshead to continue a journey to London. As well as providing Newcastle with a southern rail route, it enabled the busy road traffic of the day to avoid the steep slopes of Dean Street and Side, which the horses found difficult, especially with a heavy load to pull.

The first pile was driven in 1846, with the bridge being opened in August 1850, and the Central Station received its first train from the bridge in 1851. Counting the materials, labour and land purchase, the bridge cost the then staggering sum of £491,000, a price, which it is thought only the railway companies could have financed. Some of these costs were recovered by the tolls charged on the bridge such as thruppence (3d, just over 1p) for a single-horse carriage and a halfpenny (1/2d, less than a quarter of 1p) for a pedestrian.

The bridge had a revolutionary design for its time, with trains running on the top deck and a road running underneath. It was also the first bridge built with both cast and wrought iron as it has six spans of cast iron arches tied with wrought iron strings supporting the railway some 40 metres above the River Tyne. Road traffic first crossed the bridge on the 4th February 1850 and in 1922 the road deck was strengthened to take the increasing number of tramcars.

The bridge is less important today, as now all the mainline trains cross over the Tyne using the King Edward VII Bridge and tramcars are no more. The trains and road traffic that cross the High Level Bridge today weigh many times more than the traffic when the bridge was opened, yet the bridge is still almost entirely in its original condition and is still used by pedestrians today to cross the river. The only major change is that the number of rail tracks have now been reduced to two.

On 2nd August 1869, an accident happened on the High Level Bridge, which resulted in the death of Mr Robert Heads, of Simpson Street, a traveller for Messrs. T. & W. Smith, ship-builders. Two of the carriages being overturned after leaving Gateshead Station caused the accident. At the inquest, there was not sufficient evidence to show how the carriages got off the line.

On 7th June 1849, the Mayor of Gateshead, Mr Hawkes, a partner of Messrs. Hawkes, Crawshaw & Co., the contractors for the ironwork of the bridge drove the last key of the High Level Bridge into place, thereby closing the arches. Afterwards the Mayor and a number of friends dined together at Miss Murray's Half Moon Inn to commemorate the occasion, and the men working on the bridge were plentifully regaled with strong ale.

The High Level Bridge

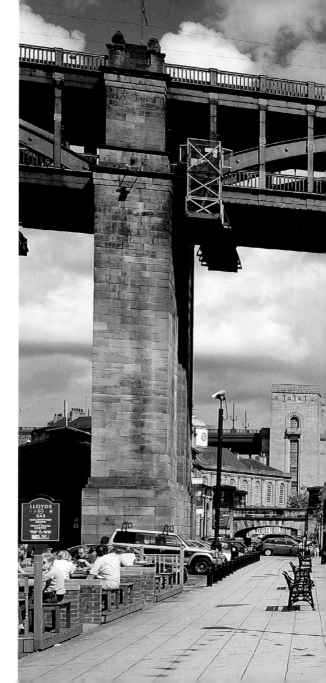

HIGH BRIDGE,
AND OTHER BRIDGES

The word bridge plays an important part in Newcastle's history. In some forms it is obvious, such as the Tyne Bridge, and so forth but there are others that have gone forever.

By the Watergate where the high crane once stood in the days before the docks were built downstream, the ships would lie some five to six deep as they did all the way along the quayside. This particular mooring being the first, was called the Bridge Tier, but alas the forests of masts have gone forever and the name only remains in historical texts.

Bridge also crops up in one or two of Newcastle's street names, betraying the fact that the city is built on the deep ravines and valleys of several streams. One of these thoroughfares is High Bridge, now split in two by Grey Street, which connected Pilgrim Street with the Bigg Market.

Its name comes from the time when the Lort Burn ran open to the sky and was crossed by the Upper and Nether Dean Bridges. High Bridge marks the site of the Upper Dean Bridge and the street still gently dips down to the valley of the Lort Burn. It is said that the actual position of the bridge was situated outside numbers 31-37. The Lort Burn was described by contemporary writers as 'a vast nauseous hollow' and 'a place of filth and dirt'.

Besides the Lort Burn, the other notable stream flowing through the city was the Pandon Burn that flowed to the east of the town on its way to the Tyne. The Great North Road crossed this stream via the bridge at Barras Bridge near where the Hancock

Museum is today. As the traffic increased, this bridge was widened in 1819 but the writing was on the wall and the valley was filled in and the bridge covered over.

Further down its course the Pandon Burn's ravine hindered the development of communications in an easterly direction causing much congestion. Therefore, a new bridge was built in 1812, to alleviate the problem and the street leading to it became known as New Bridge Street. The bridge was a tall structure with two graceful arches but was demolished in the 1880s when the burn was filled in.

In the 1880s W. Owen opened a pharmacy in Barras Bridge. Behind the shop was a mineral water factory known as the 'Lemonade Factory'. Here Owen produced ginger ale, lemon squash and sparkling tonic water. An airshaft for the Metro is now in the spot where Owen's pharmacy once stood.

High Bridge
Opposite: The High Level Bridge

THE REDHEUGH BRIDGE

The name Redheugh is said to come from the steep bank here, the heugh, and the local reed beds. However, the story of the first Redhuegh Bridge is not a happy one, starting with the fact that it was designed by Sir Thomas Bouch, engineer of the ill-fated Tay Bridge.

Even during its construction, the bridge encountered tremendous difficulties, one of the arches collapsed and it got worse when, on January 7th 1871, most of the scaffolding was dislodged and carried out to sea by drifting ice on the river. For some unknown reason the work force was too small to get the bridge's construction moving at an acceptable speed and in some weeks it is said there were as few as 17 men at work on the bridge.

Once the bridge was opened, traffic paid a toll to cross but the owners needed to keep their finances coming in and as a result thought up some ingenious money-making ideas. For example, in 1887 spectators were charged sixpence to stand on the bridge and watch HMS Victoria pass underneath on her way downriver from the Elswick yard.

The first bridge was demolished and the second structure opened in 1901 but by 1934 concern had grown that it was not strong enough to carry the new double-decker buses. Its approaches were also thought not to be sufficient to deal with, in the long term, the increasing volume of traffic. The bridge got in one final act of revenge as it cost approximately £2 million to demolish it!

Unlike the last bridge, the present high span pre-stressed concrete road bridge is said to have a use for the next 120 years. It was built during 1982-3 and was opened by Diana, Princess of Wales, in 1984, forming a smooth traffic access from the south into the centre of the city and now joins the new St. James' Boulevard.

The bridge is graceful to the eye, formed by the central span of 160 metres and the two side spans of 100 metres each, but pedestrian and motor traffic still suffer when high winds swooping down the Tyne Valley force the bridge to close.

The Redheugh Bridge (in the foreground).

QUEEN ELIZABETH II BRIDGE

Until the building of the Gateshead Millennium Bridge, the Queen Elizabeth II Bridge was the latest construction to cross the Tyne, being opened by Her Majesty the Queen in 1981. It is something of an enigma in terms of the river's bridges, as it seems so fragile when compared to both the larger and heavier looking Tyne Bridge and King Edward VII Bridge. However, it could be argued that the bridge plays just as an important part in the city's life as it deals exclusively with local trains, even if the volume of traffic it carries may be nowhere near as great as its neighbouring bridges. Like the King Edward VII Bridge, it became necessary because of the growth of local traffic and a need to connect the Metro system with the communities south of the Tyne.

Both a tunnel and suspension bridge were considered first. Many now think it a good thing that neither succeeded in getting off the drawing board as the bridge with its pale green hue has gained many devotees in its short life.

Unlike its neighbours, the bridge was not built on site in totality. The sections were constructed away from the site, transported here and then like some giant 'Meccano' kit were bolted together into position. The final joining in the centre took place in August 1978.

The Queen Elizabeth II Bridge may not be the most elegant or best-loved of the Tyne bridges but is still very important, simply because it offers fast and comfortable travel for the city's inhabitants for commuting to work or recreational visits to the Gateshead Stadium, the coast at South Shields, Sunderland and the surrounding areas.

The Queen Elizabeth II Bridge

THE KING EDWARD VII BRIDGE

The King Edward VII Bridge came about entirely because of the explosive growth of the railways from the late nineteenth century. The High Level Bridge took all the traffic, sometimes as many as 800 trains a day, but it brought trains only into the east side of the Central Station. This meant there was no through running service for the London to Edinburgh line and a long reversing manoeuvre back over the bridge had to be carried out. Therefore, the creation of a new bridge entering the station from the west solved both these problems.

It is perhaps an arrogance of our own time that we often forget the ingenuity and strength of the workers who built our ancient monuments as well as the appalling conditions in which they worked. The three piers that the bridge stands on were built in caissons, a strong steel case for keeping out the water while the foundations were laid. The caissons were filled with compressed air whilst 150 men dug deeper and deeper, excavating the mud and gravel. They were only allowed to spend four hours at a time on their shift. Eventually, when the site was ready, concrete was poured in, to the level of the riverbed.

The construction of the bridge was also marked by the innovative use of an overhead cable system stretched out between the two banks. It carried an estimated 23,500 tonnes of building materials and must have saved hundreds of thousand of pounds from being added to the £500,000 building costs.

King Edward VII, himself, opened the Bridge on 10 July 1906. From here is what must be regarded as one of the finest views, all the city's bridges to the east and a superb general view of Newcastle itself.

Crossing this Bridge evokes a feeling of 'coming home' to many people who live here and for this reason alone grateful thanks to those men who designed and built what is often called Britain's last great railway bridge.

The King Edward VII Bridge. In this view the second of seven bridges over the Tyne

SCOTSWOOD BRIDGE

Immortalised in the 'Blaydon Races', where it is referred to as the 'Chine Bridge' and close to the western boundary of the city, the Scotswood Suspension Bridge resulted in the building of Scotswood Road as both were constructed by a private company.

Nearly six and a half kilometres from the city centre, the bridge was built in 1831 and designed by John Green with dignified stone entrance arches. Eventually Newcastle Council bought the bridge and the road in 1905 for £36,500 and in March of that year, the toll charges ceased on both the bridge and road.

From being one of the most successful bridges it gradually entered a period of decline, because of this by 1961, the crossing speed was limited to 16 kilometres per hour. When the new Scotswood Road Bridge was opened in 1967 the old bridge was demolished, a great shame as photographs show it to be a graceful construction with simple elegant lines, reminiscent of Telford's Menai Straits bridge.

The need for a new bridge was getting desperate and in 1960, the building of a bridge 91 metres west of the suspension bridge was agreed upon that made provision for six carriageways at an estimated cost of £1.5 million.

When finally opened, the new bridge had four lanes of traffic and also carried gas, water, sewage mains and telephone cables. Problems were found with the bridge in the early 1970s and traffic was restricted to a single lane in each direction whilst strengthening work was carried out, with additional repairs being made in 1980 and 1983.

The overall total cost of the bridge was some £2.5 million but once the Blaydon Bridge was built to carry the Western By-pass over the Tyne, the bridge had its trunk road status removed and was closed whilst further repairs were carried out. The bridge is still in use today giving access to Blaydon and the Gateshead Metro Centre on the south bank.

The original bridge was one of the earliest suspension bridges in the world and the honour of being the last people to cross it went to the civic dignitaries attending the opening of the new bridge, or so they thought. They were, however, thwarted in this by a 10-year-old boy who sneaked across on his bike behind the official party.

The Scotswood railway bridge now stands disused, but like the road bridge, it has a chequered history. Built as a wooden bridge in 1839 it burned down in 1860. This was replaced by another wooden structure a year later. A single-track bridge replaced it ten years further on when a metal double track replacement went up and it was strengthened in 1943. The last train ran over the bridge in 1982 and today the bridge still crosses the river, silently suffering from the ravages of time.

During the Regatta held on the 15th September 1834, the banks were packed with spectators and the waters from King's Meadow to Scotswood Bridge were crowded with vessels of every description: steamboats, pleasure-boats, wherries and other craft; but the most conspicuous were the splendid Corporation and Trinity House barges. The Newcastle Journal reported that 'on Scotswood Road was a long line of carriages filled with the beauty and fashion of the town and district'.

Opposite: Scotswood Bridge

GATESHEAD MILLENNIUM BRIDGE

With the building of the Gateshead Millennium Bridge, affectionately known as the 'blinking eye', a new popular pastime has appeared in the city. The bridge creates a circular promenade in conjunction with the Swing Bridge that allows people to savour and appreciate both of the revitalised banks of the river. The bridge uses a variety of lighting techniques to highlight and enhance its unique design features; as well as the pathways, separate sections of it can be illuminated in hues of different colours, making this an attractive evening walk.

Costing around £22 million the bridge was opened in September 2001. The headroom for ships is 25 metres equal to the clearance of the Tyne Bridge when it is raised up and when closed the clearance is 4.7 metres, equal to that of the Swing Bridge and the navigation channel is 30 metres wide. Amazingly, the bridge can be raised and lowered, almost silently, in just four minutes.

Where it succeeds visually is that the arch blends in with the arch of the Tyne Bridge, the pair complementing each other. Another great success story is that it has brought together the two riverbanks, not just physically but also emotionally and spiritually, as it has contributed to the creation of a rejuvenated area for people to enjoy, boosting both Gateshead and Newcastle's tourism figures in the process.

In November 2000, the bridge was taken from Wallsend to Gateshead by the floating crane 'Asian Hercules II', one of the world's largest vessels of its type. Just how large can be illustrated by the fact that when the jib is extended it is twice the height of the Tyne Bridge.

An estimated television audience of 100 million people watched the bridge being lowered into place with amazing accuracy as it was only one millimetre out of its required position. To allow the 40 bolts to be connected to their anchorages the 850 tonne bridge had to be held in place while the tide ebbed and finally reached low water.

The bridge, 126 metres in length, uses one arch to form a deck for pedestrians and cyclists with the second arch providing support. When closed the top arch reaches up to a height of 50 metres, almost the height of BALTIC on the Gateshead bank. The steel pedestrian walkway, complete with benches, runs alongside the perforated aluminium cycle path, and offers superb views of the Tyne and its revitalized banks.

The Gateshead quayside is a wonder of modern design and cultural development. BALTIC, a centre for contemporary art offers majestic views of the bridge and the river. Further up the Tyne is the curvaceous shining steel, glass and aluminium waves of Sage Gateshead, a Norman Foster building that caters for all tastes across the musical spectrum in concert halls and smaller performance settings. This music centre's huge windows provide excellent views of Newcastle's quayside and city centre.

There is no doubt that the Gateshead Millennium Bridge is a triumph of modern engineering and a testament to how organizations can work together forming something beautiful and functional for the benefit of all.

The Millennium Bridge is gently eased into place by by the floating crane 'Asian Hercules II'

The frame of the Millennium Bridge contains enough steel to make over 60 double-decker buses.

The strong fender posts in the river are designed to withstand a 4,000 tonne vessel crashing into them at a speed of four knots.

The bridge lies on over 18,000 tonnes of concrete, enough to make half a million paving stones.

The Gateshead Millennium Bridge, or 'Blinking Eye' as it has affectionately been named

BALTIC

Although this is a book about Newcastle upon Tyne, it is difficult not to mention certain buildings that border the River Tyne albeit that they are on the Gateshead bank. This is especially true now that the Gateshead Millennium Bridge makes it a pleasure to stroll from one bank to the other and so, it is hard to ignore the Baltic beckoning from across the water.

Perhaps the only inhabitants of Newcastle and Gateshead who were not impressed when the work started on the new BALTIC Centre for Contemporary Art were the kittiwakes who nested on the building during the summer, making it the furthest inland colony at the time. To prevent damage to the newly restored brickwork, it was decided that the Kittiwakes would have to be evicted and so a purpose built nesting tower was erected nearby to encourage them to move house. In the first year, one hundred pairs nested in the tower. A new tower was built further down the river and is still there today.

The site was occupied from 1850 until about 1890 by the Gateshead Iron Works, but lay derelict until the late 1930s when work for the Baltic Flour Mills began in 1950. At its height the mill employed around 300 people and approximately 100 were still working there when it closed in 1980. Then the building was called the Baltic Flour Mills, owned by Rank Hovis and used as a warehouse and silo for grain and for producing flour and animal feed. Designed by Architect Dominic Williams, the £46 million project opened in July 2002 and was expected to create about 500 jobs and generate an esti-

mated £5 million a year for the local economy. The project was funded mainly through £33 million from the Lottery and the six-floor building now boasts 3,000 square metres of galleries, a cinema, a lecture theatre, workshops and artists' studios.

This large allocation of space allows the Baltic to be one of the leading art spaces in Europe for temporary exhibitions. Within its walls are artists' studios, an archive and library for both students and the public to study the ethos and development of modern art. The rooftop restaurant offers amazing views of the River Tyne and the city.

The Baltic has had quite an effect on Newcastle's art scene and has led to other ventures of a similar nature being set up. Of these, perhaps the most impressive, is the Biscuit Factory in Stoddart Street. This beautiful Victorian building has for sale a huge array of art from various disciplines including glass, photography, ceramics, sculpture, paintings and many more. Its two exhibition floors are a wonderful experience and its planned two further floors of studios, where artists may be seen working, will make it into what will surely be one of Europe's biggest centres for original art.

Above and opposite: BALTIC and The Gateshead Millennium Bridge

THE SAGE GATESHEAD

The roof of the stunning £70 million, Norman Foster, Sage Gateshead building has 3,500 square metres of glass and 9,000 square metres of stainless steel and at its highest point of 40 metres is twice the height of the Angel of the North. It is home to the Northern Sinfonia, has an extensive learning and participation programme with a music education centre, a high-tech information resource centre, and rehearsal space halls of acoustic excellence.

From this 100 metres long building, music and musical discovery is taken out into the North East and Cumbria, an area of 10,008 square kilometres. With a 1,700 seat hall and a flexible 450 seat, intimate, flexible auditorium Sage provides unrivalled facilities for all kinds of music. Around the front and sides of the building is an amazing concourse in coloured glass designed by Kate Naestry, that offers stunning views of Newcastle upon Tyne and the river.

There is enough steel in The Sage Gateshead to build a warship! You could make a destroyer like HMS Newcastle and still have enough left over to make six chieftain tanks.

Opposite: The Millennium Bridge and BALTIC.
Right: The Sage building.

61

THE TYNE

Roll on thy way, thrice happy Tyne!
Commerce and riches still are thine;
Thy sons in every art shall shine,
  And make thee more majestic flow.

The busy crowd that throngs thy sides,
And on thy dusky bosom glides,
With riches swell thy flowing tides,
  And bless the soil where thou dost flow.

Thy valiant sons, in days of old,
Led by their Chieftains, brave and bold,
Fought not for wealth, or shining gold,
  But to defend thy happy shores.

So e'en as they of old have bled,
And oft embrac'd a gory bed,
Thy modern sons, by Ridleys led,
  Shall rise to shield thy peace-crown'd shores.

Nor art thou blest for this alone,
That long thy sons in arms have shone;
For every art to them is known,
  And science, form'd to grace the mind.

Art, curb'd by War in former days,
Has now burst forth in one bright blaze;
And long shall his refulgent rays
  Shine bright, and darkness leave behind.

The Muses too, with Freedom crown'd,
Shall on thy happy shores be found,
And fill the air with joyous sound,
  Of-war and darkness' overthrow.

Then roll thy way, thrice happy Tyne!
Commerce and riches still are thine!
Thy sons in arts and arms shall shine,
  And make thee still majestic flow.

John Gibson, Marshall's 'Northern Minstrel,' 1807

Opposite: The River Tyne

Sage Gateshead - The home of music

THE SAGE NORTH PARK

Sage North Park

The Sage North Park UK at Gosforth is an incredible building housing 12,000 square metres of glass and the visual impact of this futuristic £70 million building from the A1 is simply stunning. Over one thousand of the company's Newcastle based employees work in the building, which is the first part of the £800 million Newcastle Great Park development.

This 35,670 square metre building set in 26 acres is the result of Sage's growth from a small North East company founded in 1981 to a multi-national world leader. In 2002 Sage sponsored the new music centre in Gateshead which is now known as The Sage Gateshead.

The archaeologists, who moved on-site before the builders, unearthed two full-scale Iron Age enclosures in Newcastle Great Park. These enclosures showed evidence of twelve ancient roundhouses and the settlement probably began around 750 B.C. and was occupied until about 200 B.C.

EAST QUAYSIDE

Walking eastwards along the quayside, the buildings take on a residential feel and there is a calmer air, which lacks the activity of the bars and restaurants left behind, eventually, coming to the mouth of the Ouseburn that marks the eastern boundary of the city.

At the height of trading there were no railings or chains on the riverside so that access to the ships was readily available for unloading cargo. Unfortunately this meant it was all too easy for a drunken person to fall into the Tyne and drown.

After the opening of the Swing Bridge in 1876, it was necessary to dredge part of the river, weakening the old quay and so the quay was almost entirely rebuilt between 1884 and 1886. This new quay became the busiest part of the river, extending nearly one mile to the Ouseburn. In 1910 it was further extended east of the Ouseburn.

This part of the quayside traded heavily with Danish cities, importing cereals, eggs, butter and meat products and exporting coal, cement and chemicals. Proof of this trade with Denmark can be found at the top of the slope that connects Horatio Street (previously known as Nelson Street) with Tyne Street and City Road where the former Sailors' Bethel still stands. This replaced an earlier building in Manor Chare and was a non-conformist sailor's chapel; a Sunday school was added in 1887 at a cost of £2,000. Eventually the building became the Danish Church before closing in 1949 and being converted into offices in 1991.

Tyne Street is one of the oldest roads in the east of

Moorings at the Ouseburn / Opposite: St. Peter's Basin

the city, first appearing on maps in the late 1770s. It was built as a result of the development of traffic and trade with North Shields and the inconvenience and possible dangers of driving a carriage through the Sandgate area. This broad street with genteel houses and trees was home to watermen, ship-wrights and tradesmen and was nowhere near as crowded as the tenements of Cut Bank opposite.

When a body was found in the river it was taken for identification to the Dead House that stood immediately to the east of the Ouseburn mouth. 'Cuckoo Jack' was noted for his skill in recovering these bodies and it is said that during the 1840s and 1850s he conveyed about 200 bodies to the Dead House.

OUSEBURN VALLEY

People in Newcastle are often surprised how much the Lower Ouseburn Valley has to offer in terms of open space, history and character. A former flour mill on the riverside provides a home to artists and in the adjacent building is Seven Stories, the Centre for the Children's Book. Riverside walks provide gentle strolls and the regeneration of the area has been so successful that kingfishers and otters have returned to the river.

The area was an industrial site for over 200 years with soap, glass, lead and iron all manufactured here but today potters, small businesses and even one of the country's most unusual equestrian centres all thrive. The equestrian centre's original premises were in old stables on Stepney Bank, the last remnant of the carting trade based in the area. The stables were built in 1897 for the Globe Parcel Express Company and today are used for inner city residents to learn riding and stable management.

Prominent in the valley are the three bridges that cross above, whilst you cannot fail to notice the old chimney in Lime Street from the flour mill. The ruins left from a flax mill still stand by the river, on land that was later used to manufacture white lead. The manufacturing of white lead for making varnishes and paints was very prevalent here but the health hazards were appalling and many young women died as a consequence of working in the trade. So much so, that the factories became known as the 'White Cemeteries'.

The Lower Ouseburn Valley is rapidly becoming an area that the business community are taking note of and it is envisaged that apartments and flats will gradually start to appear here too, in much the same way as has happened on the quayside but on a smaller scale. The area is already attracting more people for a recreational day out. Indeed the Newcastle Motor Boat Club has been sailing from the mouth of the Ouseburn since the 1920s.

The Ouseburn Valley and Viaducts

OUSEBURN VIADUCTS

The Ouseburn Viaducts give some idea of what Newcastle must have looked like up until the early nineteenth century when the Lort and Pandon Burns could still be seen, when they were not yet covered over and bridges still connected the western and eastern parts of the city.

The 280 metres long rail viaduct of the Newcastle and North Shields Railway soars 33 metres above the valley floor. Designed by John and Benjamin Green, the foundation stone was laid on 13th January 1837 and it was completed in May 1839. It was built with laminated timber, the abutment and piers are of stone and the five arches were reconstructed in iron in 1870. The two-tracked line became four-tracked in 1887 with the addition of a new viaduct alongside and to the north of the original.

Alongside is the Byker Metro Viaduct, 815 metres long and 30 metres above the Ouseburn. Completed in 1979, it was opened in 1982 as part of the official opening of the St. James to Tynemouth section of the Metro.

Further down the Ouseburn valley is the 334 metres long Byker Bridge, which was built to avoid the steep slopes of Byker and Stepney Bank. Pedestrians first used the bridge in 1878 and in 1879 carts and carriages also crossed the Ouseburn here. Initially a small toll was enforced but this was withdrawn in 1895.

The first passenger railway coach ever made was constructed, to Stephenson's order, by Atkinson and Philipson's of Pilgrim Street, Newcastle.

ALL SAINTS' CHURCH

Strangely enough, Newcastle had only four medieval churches, when considering the plethora in cities such as London and York, this may seem odd, but these churches are all gems in their own right and well worth a visit.

All Saints' Church is very different to the others as the building was deconsecrated in 1961, for like the nearby Royal Arcade, All Saints' was too far from the city centre, and as the homes surrounding it were replaced with office blocks it suffered from a lack of parishioners.

The present building is on the site of the medieval Church of All Hallows, which is recorded as being here in 1286. It must have been a very beautiful place in the Middle Ages, with the tree-lined valleys of the Lort and Pandon Burns sloping away either side and the views of the Tyne in front, setting it in quite idyllic surroundings.

In 1785, the structure of All Hallows was in such poor condition it was decided to build a new church on the site. David Stephenson, who had studied architecture at the Royal Academy Schools in London, had his design accepted. At a cost of £27,000, building commenced in 1786, was completed ten years later, and is considered a rare British example of an elliptical, Renaissance style church.

When the tower of the old church was being demolished, it was necessary to use gunpowder as the mortar was bonded so strongly with the stonework.

What is particularly interesting about the church is the round body giving it an almost Byzantine feel. It is entered by passing through a wonderful pedimented detached portico standing on four columns at the front of the tower.

Today the building looks more like the sort of structure you would associate with the London skyline of Sir Christopher Wren and so should be considered one of the most beautiful churches in the city.

On the top of the steeple is a stone ball and when it was set in position John Burdikin, a militiaman and afterwards a barber in Gateshead, ascended the scaffolding stood on his head on the ball with his feet in the air, and strange to say his son did the same during some repair work in 1816.

THE NEWCASTLE GENERAL HOSPITAL

The Union Workhouse in Westgate Road was opened in 1839 to care for the 'able-bodied poor', to look after 'imbeciles', pregnant women and the sick. By 1869, built behind it, were a schoolroom, bake house, dining hall, laundry and workshops. Today, the stumps of the workhouse wrought iron railings can be seen from Westgate Road and some names such as 'Bake House' are still visible, carved into the stonework opposite the Tomlinson Library entrance. It is a shame that the 'Room' of 'Sewing Room' has been obscured by a modern sign announcing 'Social Work Department' - social history hidden by social work!

A gatepost on the west side says 'Vagrants Ward' where tramps were admitted, given a bath, bed, breakfast and a pile of stones. When they had broken the stones into small enough pieces to pass through a grill they were unlocked and allowed to go on their way.

Henry Milvain proposed building a hospital here and by 1870, the Poor Law Infirmary, costing £16,302 was built. It was later known as the Union Infirmary and in 1920 as the Wingrove Hospital. Hospital plans for 1902 show a school between the workhouse and the hospital with a garden and swimming pool at the rear. The City Council Health Committee took over the hospital in 1930 naming it the Newcastle General Hospital.

In 1919, a diagnostic X-ray machine was purchased from an Army Disposal Unit at Catterick. In 1928 a training school for nurses was added with

The Newcastle General Hospital

a hostel across the road and a connecting pedestrian subway, which travelled eighteen feet below the surface of Westgate Road and carried mains services and steam pipes from the hospital boiler house. The old nurses' home is now called Angel Heights and is a hostel for asylum seekers.

In 1937, a venereal disease clinic was opened. During World War II, many troops were unable to fight due to VD. To trace the sources of these infections the Government brought in Defence Regulation 33B in 1942, which allowed doctors to ask for details of sexual partners and failure to

provide information resulted in prosecution and imprisonment. Newcastle is unique in the UK in having provided over 60 years of uninterrupted contact tracing, now called partner notification.

A regional Radiotherapy Centre opened in the 1960s and in 1995 a high security isolation unit to deal with patients with infectious diseases.

Newcastle General Hospital is now managed by the Newcastle upon Tyne Hospitals NHS Trust. The majority of the hospital is relocating to the Freeman Hospital and the R.V.I. in 2008.

THE ROYAL VICTORIA
INFIRMARY

A white marble and sandstone statue of Queen Victoria graces the front of the Royal Victoria Infirmary. It is the young Queen Victoria, standing in robes, wearing a crown and holding an orb and sceptre, who looks down kindly upon the patients, visitors and staff coming and going, to and from, this Newcastle hospital, known locally as the RVI.

To commemorate the Diamond Jubilee of Queen Victoria in 1897 funds were raised to build a new hospital in the city. A site was provided on the Castle Leazes Moor by the Corporation and Freemen of Newcastle and £300,000 was raised towards the building. Construction work began in 1900 and in 1905 the nurses' home was opened in the hospital grounds, followed by the opening of the hospital on 11th July 1906 by King Edward VII, who also unveiled his mother's statue, the work of Sir George James Frampton R.A. and a gift from Sir Riley Lord.

This new hospital replaced the old infirmary which was situated at Forth Banks, but in spite of extensions and improvements the situation became increasingly unsuitable due to increased road traffic, the railway and the cattle market.

It is indeed difficult to design a hospital to keep pace with its steadily widening range of activities and from the very beginning expansion was on the cards for the RVI. Almost immediately, in 1907, the new electrical department was opened followed in 1908 by a massage school. In 1917 an act of Parliament was passed so that three pavilions could be built on

The Royal Victoria Infirmary

Castle Leazes to help care for those wounded in the First World War. The nurses' home was enlarged in 1931 along with a new block for resident medical staff. An orthopaedic block with 48 beds, an out-patients department and an operating theatre were added in 1933.

The RVI has continued to care for the people of Newcastle now for 100 years and has expanded and changed to keep abreast of new philosophies,

knowledge and to meet the requirements of the community.

More recently, in 1998, a £3.5 million, multi-storey car park was opened with 576 spaces and a CCTV security system for the convenience of patients, staff and visitors. In the same year plans were announced in the 'Evening Chronicle' to demolish the 'Victorian Nightingale dormitory wards' and replace them with state-of-the-art facilities. At the dawn of the new millennium, the Trust closed the accident and emergency unit and moved it to the General Hospital at the cost of nearly £1 million. In 2005 it looks as if the burns unit will close with the nearest unit then being in Manchester.

Benefactors are as necessary today as they were in 1900 when John Hall and Mr & Mrs W. A. Watson Armstrong each gave £100,000 towards the building of the RVI. One of the many modern benefactors of the RVI is the Brainwave appeal set up in 1988 by Margaret Cowen which has raised over £500,000 for equipment.

The RVI has many achievements to be proud of and these must include the work of Sir James Spence, a paediatrician, who was born in Amble, Northumberland in 1892 and in 1922 took up a post at the Royal Victoria Infirmary.

In 1933 Sir James Spence was asked by the City Council to study 'The Health and Nutrition of the children of Newcastle upon Tyne between the ages of one and five years' as there was concern in the city about the increasing poverty, sickness and malnutrition as Newcastle, like many other cities, was suffering from the effects of the economic depression.

He found that over one third of the children in the poorer districts were unhealthy or physically unfit and malnourished. Further investigation showed very high levels of mortality mostly caused by infection.

In 1939, about one in every 16 babies died in the UK - in modern terms this is only seen in places such as the most deprived parts of Africa. In 1942 the first Department of Child Health in England was set up at the RVI and was headed by Sir James Spence.

Wartime conditions hampered the start of this new department but when hostilities ceased the RVI began attracting aspiring paediatricians from all over the world.

It was in 1947 that Spence, his junior colleague Fred Miller and his team began the Thousand Families Study. The team recruited all 1142 babies born to mothers resident within the city in May and June 1947 into the study. This study was certainly pioneering work and as the members of the study had a red spot placed on their GP records to identify them, they have become known as the 'Red Spot Babies'.

The information collected depicts family life in Newcastle at that time showing that 14% of houses were unfit for habitation, 33% were overcrowded, 25% did not have their own toilet and nearly half the houses had no bath. Almost every child had contracted a chest or throat infection in the first year and in all 1625 illnesses had been reported and some babies had died. The most important factor that contributed to poor infant health was poverty. The significance of the data was realised and the study was extended until the children were 15 years old and since then partial follow-ups were done at 22 and 33 years. In the 1990s, to investigate if birth weight has a direct link to health in later life, an enormous exercise was undertaken to track down the 'Red Spot Babies' and in the end over 800 were traced and followed up at age 50.

The importance of the data received from this Thousand Families Study cannot be underestimated and further follow-ups are now planned. The Thousand Families Steerng Group manages the study, but about 50 scientists and doctors are involved in researching a wide range of themes including oral health, nutrition, cardiovascular disease, mental health, aging and social inequalities. The information from this groundbreaking work at the RVI is used in research all over the world and is a testament to all the 'Red Spots' who have continued to support this study for more than half a century.

Very appropriately, construction is underway for a new children's hospital at the RVI which will bring together all the specialities and include dedicated critical care facilities for children as well as a teenage cancer unit, the children's bone marrow transplant service and the severe combined immune deficiency unit which will be one of only two in the country.

Since April 1998, the Royal Victoria Infirmary is part of Newcastle upon Tyne NHS Trust.

'Red Spot Babies' Facts

They have spent about £18.5 million on cigarettes.
They have eaten 56,000lbs of fat a year.
They have used 661 million calories a year.
Their total weight is 11,200 stones - more than half the group are classified as obese.
They have consumed 18 million units of alcohol.
Laid end to end, the group would fit round St. James' Park twice!

THE FREEMAN HOSPITAL

Purpose built by John Laing Construction and costing £15 million to build and equip the Freeman Hospital's foundation stone was laid in 1972 by Sir Keith Joseph, then Secretary of State for Social Services. The first patients were admitted in 1977 and Prince Charles officially opened the hospital in May 1978. This 800 bed hospital boasted 18 operating theatres, three acres of buildings, 400 miles of piping, over three miles of corridors, three and a half million bricks and nearly 200,000 tons of concrete.

The reception area, a far cry from what was usually expected in a hospital, was compared to an airport lounge as it had an attractive seating area, and most intriguingly, did not smell like a hospital due to the ventilation system. The teaching facilities were second-to-none with lecture theatres, classrooms and a library for use by the Newcastle School of Nursing.

One of the areas that has brought fame to the Freeman is the cardiothoracic centre. Starting with just two surgeons it has grown to be the only unit in the country to provide the full range of cardiothoracic surgery for adults and children including heart transplantation with the first heart transplant in an adult being carried out in 1985 and during the next twenty years over 1,200 heart and lung transplants have been performed. This is an outstanding achievement for the Freeman Hospital.

Today as you walk into the Freeman Hospital, the reception area has a wonderful semi-circular

The Freeman Hospital

reception desk that would not be out of place in an upmarket hotel and it exudes an atmosphere of professionalism and calm. On the right hand side is an interesting stained glass window, rediscovered during the demolition of the former nurses' home at Walkergate Hospital. Further along are the shops and library and turning left brings you to the Chapel of Christ the Healer with its modern stained glass windows casting a peaceful glow over this little chapel.

The League of Friends always seem to be there with their book trolleys, manning the library, helping with the shop, raising funds and being forever helpful and their contribution to the Freeman must not be underestimated.

The Freeman Hospital is managed by Newcastle upon Tyne Hospitals NHS Trust and construction is underway, with a completion date in 2008, for a new cancer centre at the Freeman along with a new renal services centre with 40 dialysis stations.

THE 1960s & 1970s

There are those who say that the 'Swinging Sixties' in Newcastle refers to the steel ball smashing into some of the finest buildings as they were demolished. The Development Review of 1963 brought massive changes to the fabric of the city, and the enormous growth of traffic, meant that pedestrianisation schemes and relief roads would needed to be developed.

One of these roads was John Dobson Street, built in 1969, as a direct attempt to reduce the traffic in Northumberland Street, which was so bad that a footbridge was erected so pedestrians could cross over in safety.

The Central Area Plan of the 60s eventually led to the office complex around All Saints' Church and the Eldon Square Shopping Centre, which swept away so much of the city's historical heritage. These two building complexes are representative of what went on in the city, replacing some of the finest buildings with concrete and brick monoliths.

The leading politician at the time was T. Dan Smith who had a vision of the city becoming in architectural terms, 'the Brasilia of the North'. Many believe that he was a visionary, ahead of his time, others portray him as something of a charlatan, trapped in a web of corruption. Smith was a keen advocate of culture and was behind a scheme to inject £90 million to make Newcastle into 'the Milan of the North'.

One of his most criticised plans was for high-rise housing. The Cruddas Park housing scheme was part of his grand plan for a 'city in the sky'. Whatever your views are of the changes to the cityscape, Smith's legacy still lives on in the streets of Newcastle.

Although the rise of the concrete jungle, in the eyes of some, is deeply regrettable, the planners of the 1960s did succeed in taking steps towards making Newcastle a modern city. In some areas affluent houses of the previous centuries had degenerated into slums and these were cleared away. Perhaps in today's more enlightened age they would have been dealt with more kindly and retained, repaired or restored as part of our heritage.

Newcastle was definitely swinging in the sixties as groups such as 'The Animals' burst onto the world stage, and 'Lindisfarne' were performing in the folk clubs.

The 1970s saw other buildings spring up replacing old terraces that had become virtually derelict. One of these areas was Byker, which had some very poor quality housing, with approximately 80% of homes lacking their own indoor toilet. These houses had been built during the 1800s industrial expansion for the workers in the heavy industries around Ouseburn and the north bank of the Tyne.

What is now known as the Byker Wall was begun in 1960 and designed by Ralph Erskine, who lived for most of his life in Sweden, and is said to have based the Byker Wall on his experience of designing housing north of the Arctic Circle. The north facing wall of the maisonettes has tiny windows and somewhat impenetrable brickwork, which was designed to insulate against the cold winds and the sight and sound of cars from the planned Byker bypass. On this side were rooms such as kitchens and bathrooms and

The Byker 'Wall'

on the other side, which had views of the river, were the main living areas. The new housing estate was completed in 1978 and was one of the first major attempts in the United Kingdom to consult the community on the design of their new estate and homes.

Today the Byker Wall is included in an official list of buildings, which includes the Barbican in London and the Dounreay nuclear power reactor, that are considered to be amongst the most innovative designs of the twentieth century.

THE MOOT HALL

Newcastle's trend in the late eighteenth century towards classical grandeur and respectability expressed itself in many ways but especially so in grandiose, classical buildings. Entire new streets were constructed such as Dean Street, which gave improved access to the quayside. Another example of this tidal wave of building is the Moot Hall, now standing in the old courtyard of the Castle, opposite the Keep.

The Court of Assize at Newcastle sat at the Guildhall and that of Northumberland sat in the old Moot Hall. The building became increasingly inadequate and in 1809, it was demolished to be replaced by the new Moot Hall, built from a design by William Stokoe, in a Greek Doric and Pediment style and is an early example of neo-classicism in the city. The southern face was built as a copy of the Parthenon whilst the northern, with its Doric portico, is very imposing. By August 1812, the building work was sufficiently advanced to allow the Northumberland Court of Assize to return from its temporary accommodation at St. Nicholas' Church.

The position of the present Moot Hall was, in the heyday of the Castle, occupied by a strong tower overlooking the Sandhill and the northern end of the Tyne Bridge. The hall approximately stands on one corner of the triangular castle yard and during Assize Week travelling companies of actors performed farces and melodramas here. In the time of Elizabeth I, there was another hall on this site and it is recorded as being called the 'Moot Hall or Hall of Sessions'.

Above and opposite: The Moot Hall

Later it was the site of the Half Moon Battery in the Civil War and the present building was used as the County Court in the twentieth century.

Across the space where once stood Henry III's ceremonial banqueting hall, directly opposite the Moot Hall, is another classical building now the Vermont Hotel. Built on the foundations of an earlier structure dating from 1910 it once served as the County Hall and opened its doors in 1934. Designed by local architects Cackett, Burns, Dick and Mackellar it is an interesting building with many attractive features, fooling one into thinking it is considerably older than it is.

Just to the rear of this building is Dogleap Stairs, the name probably derives from 'dog-loup' as before widening in the early nineteenth century it is said it was so narrow a passageway that a dog could jump or loup over from house to house.

PILGRIM STREET

Looking at Pilgrim Street today it is difficult to imagine that originally it was a narrow lane from Side via Akenside Hill, along which pilgrims walked along on their way to visit the Shrine of Our Lady of Jesmond, now called St. Mary's Chapel. There was even a Pilgrims Inn, close to the top of the street to give them accommodation and refreshment, whilst in the seventeenth century every Tuesday and Saturday a market for rye and wheat was held here.

At the top of the street stood Pilgrim Gate that gave access to the city through the walls. It was an incredibly strong defensive structure, so much so that when it was captured from within during the siege of 1644 the Scots outside fired on their own men who were calling them to come in, as they could not believe it had fallen. It stood until 1802 when it was deemed too narrow for the traffic and was consequently demolished.

Pilgrim Street is the site of many treasures, not least is the Northern Goldsmiths' building with the Golden Lady on the clock, a famous meeting place in the city. Designed by James Cackett, the 1890s Northern Goldsmiths' building features a corner dome on a tall drum. The clock was added in 1932 by Cackett, Burns, Dick and Mackellar and the delightful Golden Lady by Alfred Glover. The red dome houses a peal of bells that are linked to the Golden Lady and her clock and they chime the quarter, the half and the hour. Behind the clock, a bay window projects out into the street. The large shop window is original and because the workrooms above needed extra light, the building has a high percentage of windows. The shop has a wonderful interior with its sweeping balustrade and wooden and glass cabinets. Even the mosaic entrance floor in the doorway is a work of art.

At the other end of the street is Alderman Fenwick's House, a masterpiece of modern restoration and a reminder of the wealth of the city's merchants in days gone by.

Between these two buildings is the fascinating Market Lane public house that looks much older than one would think. Today, with its peeling paint, revealing the lovely brickwork below, it looks an average city building, but it may have been a residence of some quality as it has stone columns on its front face. Market Street is a product of Grainger's new developments. Worswick Street is named after the Reverend James Worswick who founded the first Roman Catholic Chapel in the city after the reformation, in Pilgrim Street in 1798. Redevelopment has left its mark on the street with Grainger's Royal Arcade being swept away, although there is a bar there that gives you some idea of its majesty.

It is at the northeast corner of the street where the greatest tragedy, certainly in visual terms has occurred. Here is the decaying Odeon cinema, in its time one of the finest Paramount theatres in the UK. The Odeon's final evening was on 26th November 2002 and its future is still uncertain, while its facade could well be retained as part of any re-development, it is for its 1930s Art Deco interior that the building is most famous.

Beside the cinema, jutting out into the street is one of the most visually disappointing buildings in

The Northern Goldsmith's clock, on the corner of Pilgrim Street and Blackett Street

Newcastle, completely spoiling the view southwards from Northumberland Street. Supported on two pillars it is a grey concrete office block that even on sunny days can look depressing, a legacy of the 60s, the building does however show the development of architecture in the city by adding to the street's amazing collection of buildings from past centuries.

Carliol House, Pilgrim Street

ALDERMAN FENWICK'S HOUSE

If Alderman Fenwick's House is not the jewel in the crown of Newcastle's architectural history then it comes very close indeed to that accolade. What is sad is that so many people do not know it even exists and walk past it every day on their way up and down Pilgrim Street.

Today several companies use the house, making it once again a thriving part of business in the city. The public areas of the house are open to parties who book in advance and going around it is a remarkable experience. The superb oak staircase rises up level after level until you reach the decorated wind vane ceiling which is connected to the vane on the roof. Fenwick was a merchant and needed to know how the wind fared for his ships and the goods they carried. Gradually as the centuries passed, Pilgrim Street lost its importance and in 1781, the house became an inn called The Queen's Head. In 1784, the accommodation was considerably enlarged and a public dining room provided meals during race week. The Queen's Head was one of several such thriving establishments in the city but it seemed to take preference for occasions such as banquets and receptions and was even used as a sales rooms and for auctions.

In the early 1880s the building was leased by the Tyne Liberal Club who made considerable alterations to the fabric of the building. Eventually the house became a gentlemen's club, a convenient place for lunch for those professional men who worked in Grey, Collingwood, and Mosley Streets.

The renovation from near dereliction of this nationally important building is a miracle and one due, in no small measure, to the hard work of Tyne & Wear Building Preservation Trust and many other organisations and individuals who worked on the project. It was one of many important buildings where the owners had applied for complete demolition and site redevelopment, but thankfully it was bought by the City. In 1980, it was leased to the Trust, which began to restore it to its former grandeur.

Alderman Fenwick's House is one of Newcastle's finest buildings with a most interesting history and the restoration, carried out by a dedicated band of people, has given the city back one of its gems.

Alderman Fenwick's House, Pilgrim Street

Interior, Alderman Fenwick's House, Pilgrim Street

THE GEORGIAN PERIOD

The Georgian period was one of incredible importance to Newcastle upon Tyne. It saw the first movement of the city away from the medieval timber-framed, cramped housing to the wide streets we see today. This period also took the city into a flowering of the arts and sciences and saw the rise, not only of town planning, but also in the development of charities and organisations caring for the sick and needy.

This was the time of the booming coal economy, resulting in other industries growing, such as shipping, as it was essential for importing the materials needed as well as exporting the coal and other products. Therefore, people moved in from the surrounding countryside to seek employment and the population in the city showed a steady increase. Middlebrook estimated the population in 1700 to be 18,000 and around 24,000 in 1770, and all were packed inside the city walls.

The Blacketts' huge mansion and others like it, contrasted with the packed tenements on the quayside; the streams of the city still ran under open skies though they were gradually turning into open sewers. The steep denes of these streams still acted as a barrier to movement around the city and even as late as 1785, High Bridge was the only street connecting the Bigg Market with Pilgrim Street because of the ravine of the Lort Burn. Communication from the quayside to the city was still via Side. It is only a short walk up to the town above, but in those days, the difference in the quality of life, the buildings, and people was enormous.

Into this city sprang what must be regarded as one of the finest group of builders and architects ever working in a city at one time. David Stephenson was born in 1756, the son of a carpenter he designed Dean and Mosley Streets and the beautiful All Saints' Church.

Newcastle's Assembly Rooms were built to innovative designs by the local architect William Newton, born in 1730. In 1768, he also designed the new St. Ann's Church in City Road, one of the finest churches in the city. Some of the stone used to build it came from the old town walls on the quayside; indeed it was in the Georgian period that the walls began to disappear at an increasing rate as the need for space and building materials made their destruction inevitable.

Summerhill Terrace

THE ROYAL ARCADE

Alas, the Royal Arcade is no longer standing. According to several writers, towards its end, the building had the appearance of a 'smoke blackened pseudo-classical department store'. Yet with its Greek columns, pediment, handsome vaulted ceiling and eight glass domes many regarded it as one of Richard Grainger's masterpieces.

Grainger had originally intended to build a corn exchange on the site in Pilgrim Street but his plans were not acceptable to the corn merchants, so he changed it to a commercial and shopping arcade instead. Amazingly, it took only a year (1831-32) to build at a cost of £45,000, from a design attributed to Dobson but there is a suggestion that the designer may have in fact, been Thomas Oliver.

The demise of the Royal Arcade could be seen as a tragedy as a local newspaper, at the time of the opening, reported on the 'magnificence of the building', the 'splendour of its front', the 'beauty of its interior', the 'chequered marble pavement', 'a conservatory with Medicated Vapour' and the 'warm and cold baths'. This splendid arcade also boasted a beadle in gold braid and cocked hat pacing the pavement outside. Unfortunately, due to the Royal Arcade's position, it was not likely to succeed as a shopping arcade. The opening of Grey Street, Grainger Street, and later Northumberland Street made them far greater attractions. Eventually, the Arcade slipped into decline and once the General Post Office moved, its shops began to close and be replaced by warehouses. It then was mainly used as a short cut to the Manors Railway Station.

In the 1960s, Swan House and the massive roundabout were built sweeping the Arcade away. The Swan House building was quite an interesting construction, built by Sir Robert Matthew and Partners between 1963 and 1969, it contained a very clever variety of contrasting decks and underpasses and was originally built as the base for the General Post Office Telecommunications, now BT. When BT no longer occupied the building, it remained empty for some time before being refurbished and renamed. As 55° North, it is now a very desirable address with exclusive apartments and penthouses, benefiting from superb views over the city and river. At street level inside Bar 55°, a hint of the lost grandeur of the Royal Arcade may still be seen.

Bar 55°

THE CATHEDRAL CHURCH OF ST. NICHOLAS

The Cathedral Church of St. Nicholas is one the most memorable sights of the city from its red and gold clocks to the splendid lantern tower of the style known as 'Scottish Crown' representing the crown of thorns at its peak.

Across from the western door of the building is a panelled wood screen commemorating the regiments and men from the area who fought in the First World War. As you walk around the building it is the names associated with the history of Newcastle that are waiting to be discovered. Paramount amongst these is the monument to Admiral Lord Collingwood, Nelson's second in command at the battle of Trafalgar, who was born near-by in Side and died at sea in 1810.

The first church on this site was built by the Normans but suffered terribly from fire in the first half of the thirteenth century and was consequently pulled down and replaced with a new building. In 1448, the Lantern Tower was added to the church so as the city's wealth increased, so did the grandeur of St. Nicholas' Church. After the dissolution, the Church declined and in the late eighteenth century, it received a much-needed restoration.

John Dobson remodelled the east wall in 1859 and inserted the enormous perpendicular window, and the Church became a Cathedral in 1882. In the 1930s, death-watch beetle had eaten away much of the roof and the stonework needed repairing.

Behind the Cathedral is Amen Corner, so named because when the Cathedral's clergy held their processions around the building praying as they went, they halted here, and ended their prayers with 'Amen'. In the south east corner of the churchyard is the site of Thomas Bewick's workshop, commemorated by a bust and a plaque.

St. Nicholas Cathedral

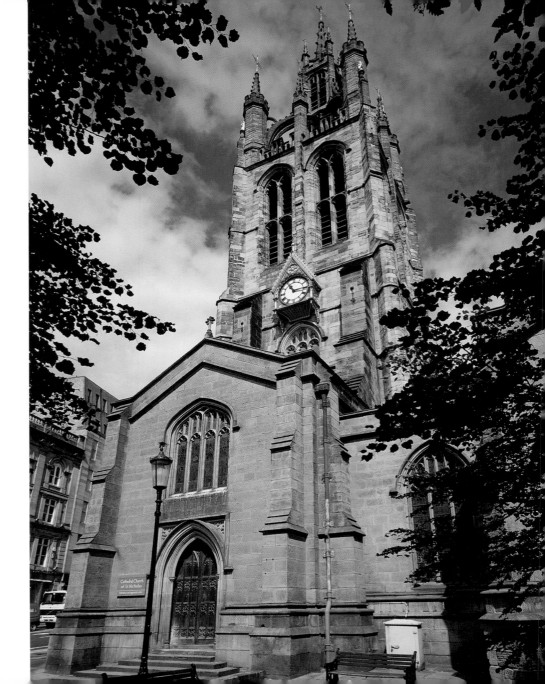

'The Vampire Bunny', St. Nicholas' Buildings
Opposite: St. Nicholas' Cathedral interior

In St. Nicholas' Square, beside the Cathedral there is a bronze Art Nouveau statue of Queen Victoria by Alfred Gilbert, the sculptor of Eros in Piccadilly Circus in London.

Perhaps the strangest part of the Cathedral and indeed one of the strangest sights in the city is the famous 'Vampire Bunny', which is found in the east side of the churchyard above the doorway into the Cathedral buildings. With its red almost demonic eyes, teeth and claws, the rabbit seems to be jumping out of the building. Although it is often referred to as a rabbit, it is described as a hare in the listed sculptures book and indeed, it does have the large ears of a hare.

Joseph Barber, bookseller, started the first circulating library in Newcastle at his shop at Amen Corner.
The north-facing clock dial was first lit by gas at 5.00pm on the 5th December 1829.
The Lantern Spire, built in 1448, has for over five centuries been a navigation point for ships using the River Tyne.

The Turnbull Building
Opposite: St. Nicholas Cathedral

THE TURNBULL BUILDING

In the future, when the Turnbull Building in Clavering Place is mentioned in any book on the history of Newcastle upon Tyne it may not be because it is an ideal industrial conversion of a Victorian building that had previously been a print works and a warehouse. Its fame may now lie in the fact that Newcastle's first flat valued at over a £1 million is in this building. (*see previous page*)

THE CENTRAL EXCHANGE & THE CENTRAL ARCADE

One of the delightful gems of the city is the Central Exchange building, probably designed by Walker and Wardle, built by Richard Grainger and completed in 1838, originally intended as a corn exchange but turned down, even as a gift, by the Corporation of Newcastle and the merchants. Discovering the Central Exchange building is an unexpected pleasure. The corners are an adaptation of the Temple of Vesta at Rivoli with a dome resting on an almost circular ring of Corinthian columns. Look closely too at the top of these domes with their copper Prince of Wales feathers drooping down over the tops. The large triangular building is quite impressive but its full majesty does not become apparent until it is looked down upon from the top of Grey's Monument. It's only then that the complexity of the building can be seen with what looks like a high terrace of almost medieval buildings with chimney pots that are invisible from street level. Interestingly it can be seen that all the chimney pots on the Grey and Grainger Street sides have been removed.

In 1870, the Central Exchange re-opened as an art gallery with a commercial exhibition area and a subscription newsroom, which was so popular that by 1890 the newsroom boasted a membership of some 2,000. A magnificent glass dome poured light onto the floor of the newsroom, which had a reputation as a plush private club for ladies and gentlemen with lounges, coffee rooms, and telephones. As times changed, the newsroom eventually became a Vaudeville theatre.

On the Grey Street and the Market Street side there was the Central Exchange Hotel, considered a well-appointed good class family hotel with 50 bedrooms. The hotel survived the disastrous fire in 1901, which left the Central Exchange severely damaged resulting in a redesign by Joseph Oswald & Son. At this point, the whole building was refurbished and the present shop lined arcade came into existence with three new entrances and extensive use of faience tiles from Burmantofts of Leeds.

These tiles can be seen below the beautiful glass barrel-vaulted roof that floods the interior with light. These ceramics are in shades of yellow and brown, with large panels, little niches, beautiful lettering, and perhaps it could be said, rather ugly animal heads.

Above the shop fronts, run two galleries with beautiful iron railings, and higher up, above the windows, there are fine ceramic fans. The fans and niches, bordered by a classical pillar design, are reflected at both ends of the arcade. It's also worthwhile examining the three entrances to the arcade with their carvings and lettering, There is a fourth, much smaller entrance in Market Street that was and still is used as a goods entrance and for the collection of waste.

The arcade is often referred to as the Windows' Arcade as the music shop J.G. Windows has been here since 1908 serving the city in a number of musical ways including selling tickets for concerts or obtaining sheet music.

Grainger originally included select apartments in the design of the Central Exchange and today with modern apartments, some of which have a private roof terrace overlooking the arcade make this a much sought after city address.

The Arcade also houses Newcastle's excellent Tourist Information Centre, which has won awards for the service it provides to visitors and locals alike.

Opposite: The Central Arcade

BIGG MARKET

The Bigg Market has always been the place where the people of Newcastle upon Tyne seek entertainment and relaxation. It gets its name from the sale of bigg, a kind of barley, and is the oldest market in the city, dating back to Norman times.

In fact the whole area of the Cloth and Groat Markets (groats being oats without husks) still carries on the tradition of entertainment today. At the bottom of the Groat Market is where you'll find the Black Boy, a pub frequented by Thomas Bewick. He also visited The Sign of the Cannon, in the Flesh Market (as the Cloth Market was then called) where literary clubs would meet before the Literary and Philosophical Society was formed.

This bustling area has played its part in putting Newcastle on the map as being one of the top cities for a night out. With around twenty pubs in this area alone, this is where young people flock in their thousands at weekends. There are also numerous eating places, especially Indian and Italian restaurants close by.

Originally there were three streets extending south from the Bigg Market, Groat Market to the west, Cloth Market on the east and between them ran Middle Street also called Union Street.

The old Town Hall, built in the 1860s, stood on a site at the top of this street but has now been replaced by a modern office block. The Corn Exchange of 1839 was incorporated into the Town Hall with its council chamber and offices, as well as a concert hall seating about 3,000 people.

Originally, the Bigg Market extended from the end of Nuns Lane down to Pudding Chare whilst the Wheat Market was found at the bottom of the hill, in the square in front of St. Nicholas' Cathedral. The Wool Market was held a little above the end of where Collingwood Street is now and still further down at the end of Denton Chare was where you would have found the Iron Market.

Another important event held nearby in the Corn Market was the equivalent of today's Job Centre where employers came to hire single servants. Young people from the countryside used to flock into the Corn Market wearing green branches, this being a symbol of their looking for employment. It must have been quite a sight watching them haggling with their future masters over their pay.

The Cloth market is also famous for Balmbra's, the renowned music hall, which is perhaps best known as the place where on 5th June 1862, Geordie Ridley first sang his rendition of the 'Blaydon Races'. At that time, the building was called the Wheatsheaf Inn, a public house with a 'built-in singing room'. and the landlord was John Balmbra who was such a notable character that the building was often called after him, hence the wording in the song. He also ran the Victoria Music Hall in Grey Street and this enabled him to live in a large mansion in considerably more comfort than most of his patrons. In 1865, the singing room was enlarged and the building became known as the Oxford Music Hall. With the rise of the Moss Empire Theatres, Balmbra's reverted to licensed premises, becoming known as the Carlton and the Gaslight and Laser before changing to Balmbra's, as it is known today. However, in 1962 it was used

Above: Balmbra's. Opposite: Bigg Market

again as Balmbra's Music Hall in connection with the centenary celebrations of the Blaydon Races.

The drinking fountain, dated 1894, at the top of the Bigg Market was originally sited in St. Nicholas' Square, but was moved from there in 1903 to make way for the statue of Queen Victoria. It carries the legend 'Water Is Best' on a shield on one of the panels!

MILBURN HOUSE

Alderman J. D. Milburn bought the site of the Robinson's print works, after it was destroyed by fire and built Milburn House in 1905, the year he was created a baronet. Bewick's workshop in St. Nicholas' Churchyard and Collingwood's birthplace in Side were destroyed in the process. Milburn House was one of the largest commercial office developments in Tyneside and provided spectacular offices for the Milburn enterprises with surplus accommodation for rent.

Sir J. D. Milburn, born in Blyth in 1851, was not only involved in the business of shipping, but was also chairman of the Ashington Coal Company and a founder of the Newcastle and District Electric Lighting Company.

He presented several pictures to the Laing Art Gallery and was chairman of the gallery's committee. This enthusiasm for artistic design influenced the construction of Milburn House and many points of interest such as the mosaic design and gesso work were his suggestions. Unfortunately, he died in 1907, just two years after completing Milburn House.

Built on a steep slope in the angle of Side and Dean Street, Milburn House has entrances on many levels. Inside it is richly decorated with light wells, stairwells, corridors, glazed screens, panelled walls and stained glass windows depicting the city guilds' coats of arms. As the Milburns were shipping magnates the building was designed in the style of a luxury ocean-going liner with the floors named in the same manner as the decks on a ship, with the top floor being 'A' , working down to 'G' on the ground floor.

In 1849, at the age of 23, William Milburn became part owner of the schooner 'John Twizel' and within three years he operated three barques carrying coal out of Newbiggin and Blyth and the London Gas, Light & Coke Company were one of his prestigious customers.

In 1867, with four new steamers, Milburn ventured into the China tea trade. These faster vessels brought home the first crops at prime market rates. Out of the tea trade season Milburn's ships transported cargoes to Australia and New Zealand. Eventually passengers were also carried on these routes. Wm. Dobson & Company built 'Port Caroline' in Newcastle in 1889. Her passenger accommodation was lit by carbon-filament electric lighting and included the added luxury of a ladies' boudoir, a music room, a smoking room, and the services of a surgeon and a stewardess. The third class was described as unrivalled and prospective travellers were encouraged to come on board and inspect the facilities when she was tied up at London Docks.

The London office opened in 1879. His son, John, later to become Sir John, who built Milburn House, handled the business in Newcastle.

By 1894, the Milburn Line boasted a fleet of 27 ships. The collier 'Woodhorn', owned by the Ashington Coal Company kept the London sailings bunkered.

After the death of Sir John in 1907, Sir Charles carried on as a partner in the firm. In 1912, the company negotiated an agreement with the Government of the State of Victoria to carry

Milburn House

emigrants to Melbourne.

Milburn House depicts the magnificence and enterprise of the Milburn shipping family who in just over fifty years turned part ownership of a schooner into a wealthy family business comprising many interlinking enterprises in coal, shipping, shipbuilding, electric lighting, and sponsorship of the arts.

THE LITERARY AND PHILOSOPHICAL SOCIETY

The present building housing the Literary and Philosophical Society opened its doors on the 18th July 1825 with the library possessing some 8,000 volumes, and this has increased to over 140,000 today.

You cannot fail to be impressed when entering this internationally famous library. Whilst walking around you get a feeling of a subtle amalgamation of Doctor Who's Tardis and The British Museum as the rooms open up around you. An impression further enhanced by the lovely, old black pendulum clock by the door that bears the legend 'Reid and Sons, Newcastle on Tyne'. The huge staircase has its walls adorned with portraits of past members, whilst the vast library room has a feeling of ornate grandeur with its plasterwork and the large glazed domes that were installed after a fire in 1893.

The library is open for anyone to join for a subscription and has an amazing collection of academic and general non-fiction books. There is also a children's library, an extensive fiction collection, and a justly famous collection of classical CDs and LPs all available for loan.

The origins of the Society go back to 1792 when the Rev. William Turner drew up an outline argument for the formation of a society for conversation, which he called 'Speculations on a Literary Society'.

The Lit & Phil, as it is affectionately known, grew out of the thirst for knowledge that was coursing through the veins of the educated classes in the

eighteenth century. On 24th January 1793, a meeting was held to discuss Turner's paper in the New Assembly Rooms in Westgate Street, where the foundation of the society was agreed, and the first committee appointed. Turner was a Unitarian Minister and regarded as the Father of the Society and his portrait by Andrew Morton is in the entrance hall, as is a marble bust by E.H. Bailey.

Many great names forever linked with the city have been associated with the Society including William Armstrong, Thomas Bewick, John Dobson, Charles Earl Grey, John Hancock, Richard Grainger and John Fenwick. On the 2nd September 1822, the Duke of Sussex laid the foundation stone of the current building. The society's records state that a sumptuous meal, 35 toasts and 53 speeches followed!

It is interesting to note also that the Society spawned other great institutions such as the Natural History Society that was formed in 1830 as a separate entity from the Literary & Philosophical Society but met in the lecture room. They stayed here until 1884 when they moved to their new home at the Hancock Museum, at Barras Bridge.

Next door to the Society is Bolbec Hall designed by Frank Rich in 1907 and built by the Society to provide an income from lettings to support its work. In many ways, the Society could be called the catalyst that formed the city, as we know it today. An oasis of quiet, it still serves the function it strived to achieve all those years ago by nurturing the intellectual and artistic development of Newcastle's population.

The Literary and Philosophical Society

 On March 8th 1830, the opening out of a female Egyptian Mummy took place in the lecture room. It was wrapped in Nankeen coloured cloth, which weighed 50lbs 6oz. The body was dissected in two hours by three surgeons and found to be in a remarkably good condition. The mummified body was then placed in a glass case and displayed in the gallery of the Library Room.

CENTRAL STATION

Above and opposite: Central Station

Much of the city's finest architecture was destroyed during the 1960s and replaced by drab concrete and brick structures. However, this is nothing new and as far as the Central Station is concerned, it could be argued that this is a case of history repeating itself. The coming of the railway to the city hastened the disappearance of Medieval Newcastle. Neville Street and John Dobson's Central Station, built between 1845 and 1850, swept away a long stretch of the thirteenth century town wall. Indeed just to the east of the station's booking hall stood the West Spital Tower.

Queen Victoria and Prince Albert opened the Central Station on August 29th 1850. In preparation for this momentous event, local manufacturers were asked to extinguish their fires between 11a.m. and 2p.m. so that their smoke did not cast a cloud over the occasion. Despite these preparations, this royal visit turned into one of distinct royal disfavour. After the celebration banquet, it would seem that Her Majesty was presented with the bill and it is said that in future, whenever she passed through Newcastle city her carriage had the blinds pulled down!

Today, with nearly two miles of platforms, the station is the hub of the city's transport system. From here trains, taxis and buses carry commuters and shoppers about their daily tasks across the city and its suburbs.

In 1863, there were about 170 train arrivals and departures each day and it is estimated that around 37,000 people used the station as part of their daily routine. On Whit Monday 1899 an incredible 33,000 tickets were issued to travellers. The station had ten platforms and seven signal cabins to get them on their way.

Modern refurbishment has dramatically changed the internal appearance of the station although the amazing six huge doors with their intricate iron latticework still remain. However, we will never see the true grandeur that Dobson intended for the portico that extends into Neville Street. The present portico was added in 1863 after a design by Thomas Prosser. Dobson had originally intended it to have a colonnaded front and an Italianate tower, a truly magnificent sight had it ever been built. To many the beauty of the station is the magnificent iron worked roofing which was unique in its time.

Behind the station is another example of the public art found in the city. The huge robotic man clutching a forge hammer represents Vulcan the God of the Forge who made things of beauty; somewhat appropriate, as nearby in South Street stood Stephenson's locomotive workshop.

THE INTERNATIONAL CENTRE FOR LIFE

The International Centre for Life, one of the most modern buildings in the city, stands on the site of Newcastle's old Infirmary which was opened in 1773 and finally demolished in 1954. The Centre opened in May 2000 and is the country's first biotechnology village, fostering advancement in the life sciences. The award-winning architect and urban designer, Sir Terry Farrell, designed the building and it offers a unique, stylish, colourful and architecturally striking setting for the International Centre for Life and creates Newcastle's new Times Square forming an open space for events and recreation.

In the middle of this space sits the original Cattle Market Keeper's Office and Toll House built in 1841 and designed by John Dobson. Amazingly, the two buildings seem to sit well together. Amongst these steel structures is another example of public art in the city. The 4.5 metres high DNA Spiral by Charles Jencks, is made from galvanised steel and was commissioned by the Centre in 2000. As well as being, quite simply, a beautiful example of modern sculpture, its representation of the DNA double helix perfectly reflects the theme of the entire site.

By education, research, and commercial application, the centre aims to share and interpret new discoveries as science begins to unravel human genetics. It does this by working with a range of partners in the bio-village who are involved in research, health, entertainment, conferences and education. The University of Newcastle's Institute of Human Genetics (IHG) is also based here.

One of the most popular of these partners is the Life Science Centre. By encouraging children and the adults to participate in exhibitions, it educates visitors in the origins of life, DNA and the miracle of the human body in a fascinating, educational and entertaining way. Each year from November to January, in the square, there is a very popular outdoor skating rink.

The International Centre for Life is rapidly becoming known as a place to meet, chat, and have something to eat in the bars and restaurants which form part of its fabric.

This page and opposite: The International Centre for Life

Cattle Market Keepers office and Toll House

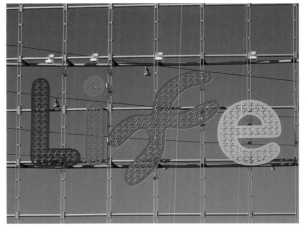

The International Centre for Life

METRO RADIO ARENA

Although it is tucked away beside the Redheugh Bridge, the Metro Radio Arena is very visible when approaching Newcastle upon Tyne by train from the south and it is one of the city's major entertainment venues.

The Arena, with over 3,700 square metres of exhibition and conference space is the only venue of its kind in the North East, and serves as a meeting place for commerce by staging various exhibitions organised by the business community.

Before the Metro Radio Arena was built, the site it occupies was derelict and was used for car parking. Previously it had been the massive marshalling yard for the North Eastern Railway goods trains. The Arena was the brainchild of the Animals pop group star Chas Chandler and his business partner Nigel Stanger, who both wanted the North East to have its own regional venue to rival anywhere else in the UK.

Opened in 1995, the building has a sprung arched roof, which from a distance, gives the impression of a massive stretched Nissen hut, but allows for an amazing pillar-free, uninterrupted space within, ideal for events. The arena is an immensely popular venue and with a stage that can be moved up and down the hall to make it from a 2,000 seat theatre style hall to its full 11,000 capacity.

It has attracted the biggest names in the entertainment world, featuring the likes of Oasis, Simply Red, Diana Ross, Elton John and Phil Collins and playing host to millions of visitors.

The versatility of the Arena as a venue is astound-

The Metro Radio Arena

ing and it is used for many events, including conferences, exhibitions, equestrian shows, basketball, ice hockey, football, snooker, wrestling, boxing, netball, shows on ice, and, of course, theatre productions and concerts.

On the 12th December, 1846 there was a great snowstorm which by the evening brought all the trains to and from Newcastle to a standstill. The next day six engines were coupled together and along with 200 excavators, but after five hours they were only reached Washington. The mail going north only got as far as Newton on the Moor where it encountered snowdrifts 20 feet deep.

St. Mary's Roman Catholic Cathedral

Rather than having one main roof with lean-to aisles, The Roman Catholic Cathedral of St. Mary has a triple roof. The cathedral was built in the Gothic Revival style between the years 1842-44 to cater for the growing immigrant Catholic population of Newcastle upon Tyne and is regarded as one of the major works of A.W.H. Pugin, who was also responsible for the interiors of the Houses of Parliament.

The Cathedral is famous for its stained glass, notably the east windows, designed by Pugin and made by the Newcastle glass-painter William Wailes in 1844, at his Bath Lane workshop. In particular, it has a wonderful modern window in the south wall that is dedicated to the memory of Private Adam Wakenshaw VC. This window commemorates the valour and self-sacrifice of the only soldier from Tyneside to be awarded the Victoria Cross in the Second World War. Private Wakenshaw was killed in action in the Western Desert and the window, designed by Cate Watkinson, uses colour and shape in a distinctly modern style to tell his story.

Also hanging in the Cathedral is the King's Colour of the 27th (Service) Battalion Northumberland Fusiliers (4th Tyneside Irish). During the Great War, some 1,900 men volunteered for the four Tyneside Irish Battalions making a complete brigade. They suffered terribly at the Somme, particularly at La Boiselle, and the Cathedral is regarded as their spiritual home.

In 2003, an underground crypt in the courtyard was discovered. After being entered, it was found that it had been sealed and covered over with grass since 1848 when Bishop William Riddell and Father William Fletcher were buried there. Both men died from the typhus epidemic, which was rife in the city, and this is possibly why the crypt was sealed. Both priests knowingly and unselfishly risked their lives by visiting and caring for the typhus victims rather than remaining in the safety of the Cathedral buildings.

Today when walking out of the Central Station, a little to your left you may notice the statue of Cardinal Basil Hume. This statue, standing in a Memorial Garden, was unveiled by Queen Elizabeth II in 2002. The three-metre bronze sculpture shows the Cardinal in his Benedictine monk's habit and stands on a stone, carved in the shape of Lindisfarne. Directly opposite the Cathedral is 36 Clayton Street West where Richard Grainger lived from 1842 until 1861.

St. Mary's R.C. Cathedral

JOHN DOBSON

There have been many fine words written about John Dobson and his immeasurable contribution to the Newcastle we know today, but without doubt, the best accolade to him is scripted in stone in Newcastle's streets.

Dobson was born in North Shields in 1787 and his talent for drawing manifested itself at an early age. He became a talented watercolour artist, engineer, and surveyor, and his architectural style helped him become one of the most famous architects of his time.

It is often said he created buildings, which seemed to meld engineering with archaeology by combining classical details with glass and iron in a way few of his contemporaries could match, an example being the roofing of the Central Station. His work as the planner of central Newcastle easily matches the designs of Georgian Edinburgh and Regency London for establishing a particular style, which has become known as 'Tyneside Classical'.

In his lifetime he produced around four hundred works; this prodigious output can perhaps be put down to the fact that he rose at four in the morning and often worked until midnight.

The results of his artistic genius can be seen all over the city, some are prominent and others tucked away, delightful gems such as the entrance gates to Gosforth Park, often unnoticed by the thousands walking through them to the races.

Some are proud monuments but all have a presence about them that tends to capture the viewer's imagination in a highly personal way.

Take for example the Tudor Gothic buildings of St. Mary's Place, not at all what many of us would expect from Dobson, but the surviving original doorways with stone steps and iron railings have a delightfulness all of their own. Those at the eastern end retain their original cellar steps.

It is not generally realised that Dobson, as well as building churches such as St. Thomas the Martyr at Barras Bridge or the parish church in Jesmond, also repaired the fabric of some of the old medieval buildings in the city such as the Keep in the Castle. He is responsible for some of the finest country houses and bridges; he even designed a heating system for St. Nicholas' Cathedral.

His gems spring up in the most unexpected places, amongst the steel and glass of the International Centre for Life is the Cattle Market Keeper's Office and Toll House, a lovely little building, which fits in effortlessly with its surroundings.

Unfortunately, many of Dobson's buildings did not escape from the demolition in the twentieth century and these include St. James' Church in Blackett Street, the Clergy Jubilee School in Carliol Square, the Forth Street Infirmary, and perhaps his finest work of all the Royal Arcade.

It is one of the great unanswered mysteries of what Newcastle would be like today if his youngest son Alexander Ralph had lived and worked in the city. He had undoubtedly inherited his father's genius as he won first prize at University College London for

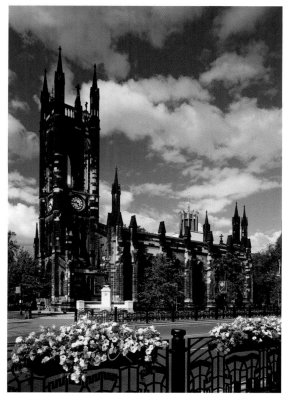

St. Thomas' Church, Haymarket

architecture in Construction and Fine Arts. He had returned to the city to work with his father when sadly he was killed in the great explosion at Gateshead, which swept away so much of the old quayside in October 1854.

Grey Street

In the eighteenth century, the Lort Burn was still open to the sky and flowed down to the river, passing the castle on its way. To build Grey Street, Grainger had to arch the burn over and fill in its valley by moving huge swathes of earth and rock to produce a flattened, level space. In fact, he had originally intended to call the road 'New Dean Street' but after Grey's Monument was erected, the street acquired its present name.

At the top of this valley, built on the site of the Old Grey Friars' Monastery, was Anderson Place, to all intents and purposes five hectares of walled country estate inside the city. It extended from Pilgrim Street to Newgate Street, came close to the town walls to the north and had Upper Dean Bridge on its southern limits.

Grainger bought the huge mansion Anderson Place and gardens for £50,000 and demolished it to make way for Grey Street and his other plans for the City. The actual site of the mansion is marked by Lloyds Bank at number 102, the building still carries on its original function when first opened, although at that time it was the Northumberland and Durham Banking Company. A plaque on the side of the building reminds us of this and that Anderson Place was where Charles I was held prisoner in 1646. He was allowed out during the days to play golf on the Shield Field.

Grey Street was described by the four times Prime Minister W.E. Gladstone as 'England's finest street', a view it's not too difficult to agree with when walking down it. Fortunately, the 1960s planners who made their mark elsewhere in the city left it alone.

Grey Street contains some of the finest buildings in the city and because of the difficulties overcome in their construction some of them are said to have foundations as deep below the ground level as they stand above!

Some of these buildings have hardly changed at all since their construction. The Central Exchange is an example of this, though the original dome structure was lost by fire. Grainger originally offered it to the corporation as a corn market but his offer was declined. In its time, it has housed a subscription reading room, coffee house, apartments, and

Grey Street at night

an exhibition gallery.

Further down the street is the Theatre Royal with its magnificent Corinthian portico. The Grainger Town partnership has done a magnificent job in restoring the city to its former glory and Grey Street shows full evidence of that. The pavements have been upgraded too, using Newcastle's original paving material, Portland stone. It is the beautiful buildings that run along Grey Street with its gently curving vista that makes it so special and developed a style known nationally as 'Tyneside Classical'.

At the bottom of the Street is the gun shop of Bagnall and Kirkwood, a direct descendant from the business of Wiliam Rochester Pape, Newcastle's finest gunsmith. What is less well known is that he started the world's first dog show, which was held in the city in 1859. There are some in Newcastle who would argue that Crufts starting soon afterwards is more than just a coincidence!

Grey Street

GREY'S MONUMENT

The Monument of Charles Grey, 2nd Earl (1764-1845) looks down over the Grainger Town from a height of some 46 metres and has done so since 1838. Earl Grey was responsible for the passing of the Great Reform Bill of 1832 that gave the vote to businessmen, merchants and gentleman farmers. Prior to this in Newcastle only the Freemen could vote, 3,000 out of a population of 53,613. The new franchise raised the number of voters to just short of 5,000. He also carried the act for the abolition of slavery in the colonies. The North East had a warm affection for Grey; on August the 24th 1832 having left London for his seat, Howick Hall in Northumberland, the Earl was enthusiastically greeted at almost every town through which he passed. Newcastle subsequently paid him a double honour. In 1836 Upper Dean Street, the finest of Grainger's new Streets was renamed Grey Street and two years later, a monument, designed by Benjamin Green, was erected at the head of it to commemorate the 40 years which the Earl had devoted to the cause of Parliamentary reform.

A little realised fact is that if viewed from Grainger Street the column is exactly central to the eye but when viewed from Grey Street it is offset; possibly this was done deliberately so as not to cause traffic congestion.

Edward Hodges Baily, who was responsible for Nelson's statue in Trafalgar Square, carved this, twice life-size, statue of Earl Grey and it was brought to Newcastle by ship from London. Few have seen the statue at close quarters, though the view from the top is magnificent and worth climbing the 164 steps.

Strangely for a commemorative statue the pedestal of the column does not have a conventional base and therefore it appears to rise from the ground somewhat abruptly. The low platform that has been built at the base has become Newcastle's main meeting place and a kind of speakers' corner. Occasionally, the air is filled with pop music from bands performing on a covered, temporary stage at the base of the Monument.

At one time there were lights on top of the Monument, which showed if there had been an accident in the town; if people were killed they were red, if the people had survived they were white.

Not many people would be aware that a lightning bolt struck the head of the original statue in 1941, which dislodged it, and it then ended up in a women's outfitters in Grainger Street. Ralph Hedley sculpted the present head in 1948.

Behind Grey's monument is the Monument Mall, a four storey shopping arcade and café court that has been designed by the Edinburgh based, Hugh Martin Partnership. Above ground, they produced a scheme to blend in with the 'Tyneside Classical' architecture at the west end with a new elevation to harmonise with the later buildings at its east end. The project has also ensured the survival of listed buildings in Blackett Street by incorporating them in the plan.

The Mall includes underground shopping links to Fenwick's department store and the creation of a new setting for the Brunswick Methodist Chapel in the rebuilt rear service lanes. The scheme received a special Landscape Design Award in 1993 from the Natural Stone Federation, presented by Prince Charles. Directly above the Monument Metro Station, a glass dome floods the interior with light.

Opposite and right: Grey's Monument

Grey's Monument, Grey Street and Grainger Street

Grey Street from Monument Mall

THE THEATRE ROYAL

By the 1760s, Newcastle society had evolved a summer season of assemblies, theatre performances and musical recitals. The need for buildings to hold these events resulted in the building of the Assembly Rooms and the Theatre Royal.

Built by David Stephenson, the first Theatre Royal opened in January 1788, in Mosley Street and entertained people there for the best part of fifty years before being demolished to make way for Grey Street. Grainger was committed to a replacement and the present building, designed by the father and son team of John and Benjamin Green, opened in 1837 with a performance of Shakespeare's 'Merchant of Venice'. This link is still carried on today with the Royal Shakespeare Company frequently appearing at the theatre.

The portico was designed to create an eye-catching building in an eye-catching street with six massive Corinthian columns rising up from enormous moulded plinths that support a classical triangular pediment bearing the royal coat of arms. Imposing it may be externally but the inside was truly magnificent as befitted a building with such grand aims. A three-storey entrance rotunda with a superbly decorated dome greeted the patrons and off this opened splendid lobbies and staircases but tragically, it was gutted by fire in 1899.

In May 1950 Miss B. Watson, a clerk on duty in the booking office, had to act fast to avert a repeat of the 1899 fire disaster. Noticing a smell of burning coming from the stalls' buffet, she dashed outside to warn a police officer on point duty who raised the alarm at nearby Pilgrim Street fire station.

The interior was remodelled in 1901 by Frank Matcham and again in 1987 by Renton Howard Wood Levin Partnership who retained Matcham's Edwardian balconies and boxes.

George Bernard Shaw had his 'Caesar and Cleopatra' given its copyright performance here in 1899, he also visited the Royal Arcade in 1921 for a production of 'Man and Superman'.

In October 1956, the soprano Evell Tomel was roundly booed at a curtain call after playing the leading role of consumptive young heroine, Mimi in Puccini's operatic weepy 'La Boheme'. A difficult role to cast, it demands a big voice from a waif-like singer. Ms Tomel earned the audience's displeasure for her literally moving death scene when the bed she was placed upon by her lover, Rodolfo, creaked, sagged and broke under the weight of her ample figure.

Over 300,000 theatre-goers visit the Theatre Royal every year for its 400 performances; in fact 84% of the Theatre's income is self-generated, possibly the highest in the area - the difference is made up by a subsidy from Newcastle City Council.

The Theatre Royal Education and Outreach (TREO) works, for the benefit of the people of the city and its environs and has over 8,000 children and adults enjoying tours, talks and workshops at the Theatre every year. They are committed to offering total access to the theatre and performing arts through a wide range of events and projects for everyone from

The Theatre Royal, Grey's Monument and Monument Mall
Opposite: The Theatre Royal by night

individuals and families to schools and groups. In the summer months, the theatre's café spills out onto the street in front of the portico whilst at night clever illuminations enhance the beauty and grace of this marvellous building.

The Theatre Royal

The beautiful interior of The Theatre Royal

BLACKETT STREET

At one time Blackett Street was one of the most elegant thoroughfares in the city. Nowadays the wall of the Eldon Square Shopping Centre borders one side of it, but there is still much to see here if you look carefully. The street was named after John Erasmus Blackett (1728-1814) who was Mayor of Newcastle four times during the eighteenth century. The Blacketts were the dominant family of Newcastle for over two centuries and John Erasmus slipped easily into the great offices of Freeman, Alderman, and Mayor.

Up until the eighteenth century, Blackett Street was a muddy lane outside the town wall leading from the New Gate to the Pilgrim Gate. When the walls were demolished the street expanded outwards, and was greatly improved by Grainger in 1824. Today the street is important as it holds within it what many people think of as one of the city's finest and best-loved buildings.

Emerson Chambers is a delightful building and benefits from having splendid, old-fashioned shop windows. It was designed by Simpson Lawson and Rayne and built at the turn of the twentieth century. This superb building, which comprises a cheerful mixture of Art Nouveau and noble baroque, was built as a restaurant, shops and offices. The present shop entrance of Iconic columns of granite with bronze decoration was the entrance to the restaurant, which was situated in the basement. The original splendid circular staircase to the restaurant sadly no longer exists, and the only remaining original feature is the ceiling.

Nearby is Parsons Polygon designed by David Hamilton in 1985, this ceramic structure acts as a ventilation shaft for the metro tunnel below. Often ignored by shoppers, it has designs pressed into clay to represent the works of Sir Charles Parsons, the industrialist and designer of the Turbinia.

Standing on the corner with Pilgrim Street is the Northern Goldsmiths' building, its clock a landmark of the city.

In 1992, the Monument Mall enhanced the street with its classical facade and glass dome fitting in well with the Grainger buildings, adding to the view that Newcastle is a city of domes and turrets.

Emerson Chambers, Blackett Street

ELDON SQUARE

In terms of architectural vandalism, there are those that argue that the destruction of old Eldon Square ranks amongst one of the greatest offences of all time. Whatever you think of that rather sweeping statement, Eldon Square was indeed a thing of great beauty and one of the finest works by John Dobson and Richard Grainger.

Photographs of the Square as late as 1949 show a peaceful tree lined square with stately classical buildings. Two sides of the square which were swept away, like so much of the city, by the planners in the late sixties and seventies.

The modern shopping centre, which took away the two sides of the original square has become an integral part of the city and with over 140 shops, including both Fenwick and John Lewis plus a huge choice of cafés and restaurants it is difficult to imagine what Newcastle would be without it.

Designed by John Dobson, the houses of Eldon Square were completed in 1831 and attracted much attention as such superior dwellings had never been seen in the north of England before.

In the centre of the Square is the war memorial, which bears the statue of St. George slaying the Dragon, the Regimental Badge of the Royal Northumberland Fusiliers. On the sides of the stone pillar are bronze reliefs of Peace and Justice and a relief of a stone lion marks the front.

The city's population was asked to donate a shilling (5p) per head to the building fund for the memorial and the target of £13,620 was very

Eldon Square

quickly reached. On 26th September 1923, Earl Haig, the commander of the British forces during the Great War, unveiled the memorial.

The road running in front of the square is Blackett Street, named after one of the most influential of all the families that shaped the city's history. Few provincial merchants had a country mansion within a town's walls, but the Blacketts, who owned Greyfriars, later Anderson Place, built up an immense fortune in the seventeenth century. It is said that Sir William Blackett and his son bestrode the town more like Renaissance princes than wealthy merchants.

The classical splendour of Dobson and Grainger's work can still be seen on the remaining side of this busy square. On a hot summer day Eldon Square can be full of people, especially at lunchtime, when city workers escape from their offices, shoppers take a break from their retail therapy and students are glad to leave behind the lecture theatres to relax and enjoy the atmosphere of this popular meeting place. Several cafés have tables outside, complete with parasols, and with the chink of china and the buzz of conversation there is quite a continental feel about this square.

ELDON SQUARE SHOPPING

ELDON GARDEN

Eldon Square Shopping Centre and the Recreation Centre were opened in 1976, covering an area of 86,397 square metres with 148 shops. In the UK's busiest shopping areas league table it ranks eighth and with Northumberland Street being tenth, Newcastle is one of the busiest shopping destinations in the country.

The shopping centre walkways echo the names of streets from Newcastle's past with two named after streets that were obliterated by its construction. High Friars remembers High Friar Lane where Richard Grainger was born. It ran almost parallel with Blackett Street from the Newgate to the Grey Friars' Monastery, which later became Anderson Place, the Blackett's mansion and is now the site of Lloyds Bank in Grey Street. Prudhoe Chare runs near the site of Prudhoe Street built in 1822 to link Northumberland Street and Percy Street. Whitecross Way is called after the medieval market cross that stood near the Newgate from the 1400s but was pulled down in 1773. The centre took away large areas of Newcastle's historic buildings but it did retain the north façade of Nelson Street.

The shopping centre is designed on two levels with the shopping malls above and a lower level providing service roads and storage areas and is itself set to change. The proposed £150 million works will provide a new bus station and Eldon Square will once again be changed with new entrances and restaurants that may bring light and life back to the bare walls of the north and west sides.

It is estimated that each year 40 million shoppers from the city and the surrounding areas spend in excess of £150 million pounds. It is therefore not surprising that specialist shopping centres have sprung up to try to capture some of this market.

The 4,087 square metres of Eldon Garden Shopping Centre was built by Greycoat in 1989, specifically designed to attract what the advertising profession calls the 'quality end of the market'. In short, it is a small, quality destination shopping mall targeting affluent, educated people between the ages of 20 and 45 and in an average week 75,000 people visit the centre.

In 2001, Peer Freeholds (Newcastle) Ltd. purchased Eldon Garden and a major expansion programme was set up. The latest five floor extension in Percy Street adds 3,000 square metres to the floor space and is another fascinating building in the city centre. It has an innovative style incorporating glass and brick that complements the walkway across the road and throws interesting reflections of light into the street itself. The designers have also made an effort to break up what otherwise would be a solid brick wall in Leazes Lane.

Linked directly to the Eldon Square Shopping Centre, the ambience of Eldon Garden is completely different, with a much more relaxed atmosphere than that of its larger neighbour. It gives the impression of being a place to eat and shop at a leisurely pace.

The Mirror Gallery, Eldon Garden Shopping Centre

Opposite: Emerson Chambers, Blackett Street, reflected in the windows of Eldon Square Shopping Centre

CHARLOTTE SQUARE

As the cultural renaissance of the eighteenth century spread northwards from London with its development of the arts and literature, it is strange that the architecture of leafy squares so well known in the capital did not repeat itself in Newcastle upon Tyne.

Charlotte Square, started in 1769, is the only example of this London style of living to be found in Newcastle. Built speculatively of substantial brick houses on three sides it had a central garden exclusively reserved for the use of the inhabitants of these houses. At one time, some of the houses were used as the Royal Grammar School. The square's occupants must have been reasonably well off and intellectually active as a list of Members of the Phrenological Association, meeting in Birmingham on 19th September 1840 denotes one 'William Cargill, merchant, Charlotte Square, Newcastle'.

In 1867, a secessionist group of the Jewish community appointed their own leaders, and founded a separate congregation, moving to new premises in the square. The grievances of the worshippers were many but in particular a surcharge on Kosher meat which proved hard on large families. The synagogue flourished and was known as the Polish Synagogue because of the many members from Poland.

The northern side of the square seems massive compared to the others because the basements use the fall of the ground to the east. When a fire burnt down number 2, the gap was left for many years. In 1982, a small housing scheme was built beyond with an archway in the gap offering views of Blackfriars at the same time.

On the eastern side of the square is the small road of Cross Street leading down to Westgate Road. Originally called Rotten Row or Ratten Rawe it has an interesting building on the corner of Fenkle Street that was one of the earliest Chinese supermarkets in the city. This area is rapidly becoming part of an expanded Chinatown as the businesses on Fenkle Street demonstrate.

Fenkle Street is shown on maps dating back to the seventeenth century where it is called Fennell Street although in 1808 its name was changed again to Charlotte Street as it ran into Charlotte Square. The present name of Fenkle Street is probably derived form the word fenkel, a northern dialect version of fennel.

WESTGATE ROAD

Westgate Road

As its name suggests Westgate Road originally ran up to the West Gate, one of the six gates that allowed access through the city walls. It has a far older connection and a glance at any map shows you immediately that it follows the line of Hadrian's Wall for some considerable distance. Westgate Road means many things to many generations of Newcastle people. Certainly, to motorcycle enthusiasts it is the place to go as quite a few of the shops along its length deal specifically with motorbikes and associated accessories.

Many of the buildings in the lower end of the street around the Assembly Rooms bear witness to the fact that during the eighteenth and nineteenth centuries Westgate Road was an extremely fashionable, residential area. Some are painted in bright red and some in yellow and above the nineteenth century shop fronts and elegant façade, the skylight windows of the servants' rooms can still be seen.

Opposite the Assembly Rooms is a statue of Joseph Cowen who was a Member of Parliament for Newcastle from 1873 to 1886. He bought the Newcastle Chronicle in 1862 when it was printed in Grey Street and founded the Tyne Theatre and Opera House in Westgate Road on the site of the Crown Inn Yard.

The houses further up Westgate Road, on the north side of the street above St. James' Boulevard, have iron railings and large front gardens. Off to the south, hidden behind the modern shops, is the Georgian district of Summerhill with its park and elegant houses looking down towards the river. On the corner of St. James' Boulevard, the road that now cuts across the street, is Blenheim House, number 145, with its huge sign on its side announcing the Robert Sinclair Tobacco Company Ltd. Built in 1913, it has an almost Egyptian look, and around the corner is the original factory and warehouse.

To other generations Westgate Road means entertainment. The Opera House has been here since 1867 offering plays, pantomimes, opera and other musical events. To yet another generation Westgate Road means the cinema. The Opera House became the Stoll Picture Theatre in 1919, as it still proclaims on its front, and where Newcastle's first 'talking' picture was shown ten years later. This part of the city was the hub of the Newcastle cinema business in its day.

THE TYNE THEATRE & OPERA HOUSE

The Tyne Theatre and Opera House in Westgate Road is one of the most important theatres in Great Britain and plays an active part in the city's live theatre scene. The theatre's name was changed to The Opera House in 2000 and there are many facilities here such as the main auditorium, bar, offices and rehearsal space that is hired out for events and functions. In May 2004 the theatre once again closed and remained so until October 2004 when a new company rented most of the building and renamed it, once again, this time The Journal Tyne Theatre.

Amongst the performers who were attracted to the theatre was Placido Domingo, as one of his major interests is theatre history. As a result, he accepted an invitation to appear in the theatre because it is such a superb example of the Victorian opera house, appearing in Puccini's 'Tosca' on 6 May 1983.

As an interesting coincidence, Sarah Bernhardt, in one of her three appearances at the theatre, performed here in 1897 in 'La Tosca', the original play by Victorien Sardou on which Puccini based his opera. The famous Harry Lauder also appeared at the theatre performing in the pantomime 'Aladdin' in 1906.

This grade I listed building has many outstanding features included in its fabric, for example, the superb acoustics, which are a result of the walls being lined with wood. The dome is also made from wood and carries the smallest whisper on stage to the far corners of the gallery. The ceiling is regarded as being very special indeed and boasts a splendid chandelier. The auditorium also retains the original triple tier of balconies and backstage an amazing system of pulleys and ropes remain that were used in the early productions for special effects.

Built in 1867 it became the 'must be seen at venue' and enjoyed a runaway success, so much so that in 1919 it became necessary to close for renovation and modernisation. It then reopened as the Stoll Picture Theatre. Ten years later, its reputation was further enhanced when the building was wired for sound with the coming of the 'talkies' and this increased its popularity even more.

The Tyne Theatre has a permanent resident in the form of its ghost called Bob who makes his presence known on a regular basis. During the 2000 pantomime of 'Aladdin', Bob appeared to stage staff on two successive Thursdays when everything went bump! Bob is said to be the spectre of Robert Courtenedge who, on the 8th April 1887, was killed by a cannonball falling on his head. The cannonball was rolled along the stage to create the effect of stage thunder, unfortunately on that night it fell off and landed on Bob.

Throughout the 60s and 70s the Stoll Picture House began to get a reputation for showing X-rated films and it eventually closed in 1974. Some three years later, it reopened with its original function of live theatre restored. On Christmas Day 1985 fire broke out backstage during a production of 'Annie' and the building was seriously damaged. Today the Journal Tyne Theatre can accommodate 1000 people in plush blue seats, and hopefully it will continue to play a vital part in the cultural and entertainment life of the city.

Opposite: The Tyne Theatre and Opera House

THE ASSEMBLY ROOMS

As Newcastle developed, the rich merchants and gentry needed a place to assemble for social occasions other than the theatre. The need arose for a building where they could hold masquerades and dances, which at the time were regarded as one of the higher forms of art.

The Assembly Rooms we know today are possibly the third that have existed in the city. The first may have stood almost opposite until about 1736 when new rooms were built in the Groat Market. Forty years later however these rooms were deemed unsuitable for a city that was on the threshold of a classical revival in architecture and social graces. A new building was needed that showed the world how important Newcastle had become.

Therefore, in 1774, to a design by William Newton, in the style of the great designer John Adam, the Assembly Rooms appeared in the city. A special Act of Parliament was needed before work could commence as the Vicar of St. John's Church held the lease on what was church property. William Lowes laid the foundation stone on 16th May 1774 and a plate with the following inscription was placed under the stone:

'In an age when the polite arts by general encouragement and emulation
Have advanced to a state of perfection unknown in any former period;
The first stone of this edifice, dedicated to the most elegant recreation,
Was laid by William Lowes, Esq. On the 16th May 1774'

The building was essentially an exercise in urban promotion, funded by both the country gentry and civic elite. The rooms are without doubt the finest original example in the country as those at Bath are a restoration after being damaged in the Second World War and those at York are far less elegant and refined.

With its sweeping staircase, green and gold furnishings, a specially commissioned carpet and seven crystal chandeliers, with the central one said to have cost 600 guineas, the Assembly rooms were billed as the largest in the country. The first floor ballroom is nearly 30 metres long and originally there were also card rooms, (card games were a great recreational pastime in the eighteenth century), a library, a newsroom, a huge supper room and, very fashionably, a coffee room.

It was here that a grand ball was held to celebrate the visit of the Duke of Wellington in 1827, which he opened with a rendition of the 'Keel Row'. The Assembly Rooms was also the birthplace of the Hancock Museum, as the meeting which resulted in the forming of the Literary and Philosophical Society was held here in 1793. The first Lord Mayor of Newcastle was knighted by King Edward VII in these Rooms in 1906.

Footnote: 1 guinea = one pound and one old shilling, £1.05p

Opposite: The Assembly Rooms

THE DISCOVERY MUSEUM

On entering the Discovery Museum, you are met by the stunning presence of the Turbinia, probably the most popular, and certainly the most impressive exhibit in the building. Her sleek lines and sheer unexpected length, leave visitors with an abiding impression of grace and speed. The Turbinia was built in 1894 by Charles Parsons and changed the face of maritime history. She was the first ship in the world to be powered by steam turbines and, in 1897, was the fastest ship in the world. At the naval review held off Spithead, in commemoration of Queen Victoria's Diamond Jubilee, the Turbinia caused a sensation by steaming between the lines of warships at a speed of 34.5 knots.

It is amazing how many of the 'world's first' can be associated with the city. Some of these can be found in the museum in Blandford Square including a model of the Mauretania, one of the most famous ships ever built on the Tyne. The Museum's 'Science Maze' interactive exhibits demonstrate a wide range of the engineering and scientific achievements of Tyneside.

The Discovery is the city's largest museum and was the first UK science museum outside London, but it has not always resided in Blandford House. Before being occupied by the Museum in 1978, Blandford House, built in 1899, had been the distribution centre for over 100 Co-operative stores across the North East and contained extensive warehouse space and offices, ideal for a museum with a large collection of objects to display. The Museum started life in 1934, in the form of the Municipal Museum of Science and Industry. The collections were kept in a pavilion built for the 1929 North East Coast Exhibition in the Exhibition Park on the Town Moor now used by the Military Vehicle Museum.

Today the Museum plays an invaluable part in the education of the city's schoolchildren with visits and courses. The 'Newcastle Story' in the John George Joicey Museum is the first permanent display to chronicle the city's history from the arrival of the Romans to our own time.

'Turbinia' at The Discovery Museum

The Great Hall - The Discovery Museum

THOMAS BEWICK

Set into the pavement between Thomas Bewick Square, just off Pink Lane, so called because of the Pink Tower on the city walls, which stood near here and Bewick Street is a large bronze replica of Thomas Bewick's engraving of a Chillingham wild bull. Bewick's cottage was situated near here, some twenty metres south-east of Cardinal Basil Hume's statue that stands in the grounds of St. Mary's Cathedral.

Reading about the life of Bewick can be a map of the city at that time, as he worked, played, and worshipped across its width. For all its grandeur, Newcastle was and still is a compact city.

Bewick's own route to work from his cottage in Forth Lane was along Westgate Street, up St. John's Lane to the Bigg Market and along the Groat Market to St. Nicholas' churchyard. He probably took these same streets home too, as his love of a jug of ale after an honest day's work was well known and as today both the Groat and Bigg Markets were well stocked with public houses. As an apprentice he lived in Pudding Chare with his aunt. He often said in later years that he lived predominantly on milk as his aunt was a widow of a Freeman of the City and she was entitled to keep cattle on the Town Moor.

Bewick's association with the Groat Market came in a number of ways but chiefly with the printing office where the first four editions of his 'History of Quadrupeds' was published, He also made a succession of heavily used blocks for the 'Chronicle' masthead. Perhaps his most enjoyable association

though, was with the Black Boy Public House, still standing today, where in 1778, he was elected to membership of Swarley's Club, which met regularly for four pennyworth of beer and conversation.

When Mosley Street was built as the first major west-east street through the old medieval town, Bewick's lodgings on the side of St. Nicholas' churchyard were demolished. He stayed here, with his younger brother John, above a dancing school where he is said to have enjoyed the fiddle playing very much indeed.

From number 45 Bigg Market, the well-known bookseller, Emmerson Charnley, distributed Bewick's works, probably while the man himself was taking ale at the Golden Lion in the Market, a few doors above the entrance to Pudding Chare.

The area around the Quayside seems to have played quite a violent part in his life as he was attacked and beaten up by three apprentice lads shortly after his own apprenticeship had started. Later in his apprenticeship, he came to blows once in Broad Garth, where he attended meetings of the radical teacher, Thomas Spence's debating society, because he failed to speak for Spence's motion.

Bewick was a member of St. John's Church but he lived on the edge of St. Nicholas' churchyard and on and off for nearly ten years and he had workshops here after leaving Amen Corner.

In 1791 he was invited to illustrate some of his bird specimens at the private museum of Marmaduke Tunstall. Several of these birds still exist and can now

Thomas Bewick's Bull memorial set in the pavement in Bewick Street.

be seen at the Hancock Museum that now holds Tunstall's collection. There is a permanent display of Thomas Bewick's life and work in the museum, as well a magnificent collection of his original water-colours and drawings.

Wordsworth called Thomas Bewick ' The genius that dwells on the banks of the Tyne'.
Thomas Bewick was born on 12th August, 1753 at Cherryburn.
When he died in 1828, he was buried in St. Mary's churchyard in Ovingham.

NEWGATE STREET

It is still possible to see the exact site of the New Gate that pierced the city walls. To the west, it butted up against the walls that form the northern boundary of St. Andrew's churchyard and on the east those that ran along what is now Blackett Street. The gate itself served as town gaol from 1400 and mostly held felons and debtors, the county gaol being in the Castle basement. Sir Walter Blackett left a generous bequest to supply the prisoners in Newgate with 'as much coal as they needed'. When it was demolished in 1823, it was replaced by a new gaol in Carliol Square.

Perhaps nowhere shows the constant evolving of the city's building sites as much as Newgate Street. The latest building to spring up here is The Gate complex with a magnificent modern building that fits in so well with its surroundings despite the difference in age and building materials. This £75 million urban entertainment centre comprising 19,330 square metres has a sky bar with views over Newcastle city centre and parking for 258 cars. The building also houses cafés, bars, nightclubs, restaurants, a casino and a 12-screen cinema. Construction work commenced in November 2000 and was completed in July 2003 by the main contractors, Sir Robert McAlpine. The architects were the William Gower Partnership, who secured detailed planning permission and Reid Architecture, the development architects. An amazing amount of materials were used in The Gate's construction, for example, after 60,000 tonnes of excavation, 30,000 cubic metres of concrete, 350,000 bricks, 800 square metres of glazing, over 1,000 tonnes of structural steel, 2,500 square metres of natural granite flooring and the acoustic ceilings and partitions measuring nearly 10,500 square metres.

Before the present building was erected, Newgate House, which was the city's earliest modern office block, had to be demolished. It too had an entertainment function as in its basement was the Mayfair Ballroom where two generations of Newcastle people spent many a happy time. Sitting snugly next door is the 1930s Art deco North Eastern Co-op Stores building with its two towers bearing the red and green neon lit barometer and clocks.

Further down the street is the Newgate Shopping Centre, built in 1969 but refurbished in the late 1990's. As it was designed for multiple usage, it included a hotel and links to existing shops. Its construction removed the crumbling Empire Palace Theatre and the Empire Cinema that had flourished for twenty years between 1913 and 1933. Still standing is the Rose and Crown Public House that has the original tiled entrances separated by a curving bay. A delightful looking building in a street that has a large variety of modern buildings.

Opposite and overleaf: The Gate cinema and entertainment complex

CINEMAS

Travelling on the Metro, at West Jesmond station, the once proud Jesmond Cinema can be seen, but it is now in a very poor state. In 1939, the city had forty-one picture houses and going to the cinema was a very popular pastime. The evolution of the cinema industry in the city came out of the decline of music halls, as can be seen by the New Tyne Concert Hall, which in 1911 installed tip up seats and began showing short films between the stage acts, as did the Hippodrome, which opened in 1913 in Northumberland Road and closed in 1933.

To many people the cinema in Newcastle means Westgate Road. The Opera House became the Stoll Picture Theatre in 1919 and was popular for many years but after a downturn it closed in 1974. The area had also become the hub of the Newcastle cinema industry, which was very important in its day. Other cinemas in Westgate Road included the Majestic, the Essoldo and the Pavilion, which started life as a music Hall in 1903 and became a cinema in 1918.

Still standing in Pilgrim Street, the 1930s art deco Paramount was taken over by the Odeon chain in the 1960's. The size of the cinema is staggering - in its heyday, it was easily capable of seating around 2,600 people. Its future is now uncertain but hopefully the building will remain. Directly opposite in Pilgrim Street, is the Tyneside Cinema, as it's known today. It opened as the Bijou News-Reel Cinema on 1st February 1937 and is the last surviving news theatre, working as a cinema in the UK. In early 1968, the News Theatre finally succumbed to the changes that television was instigating in society and closed. However, it soon reopened as the British Film Institute, supported the Tyneside Film Theatre and held its first screening on 17th March 1968. After seven years, the theatre closed and in 1976, the cinema reopened, renamed and refreshed, as the Tyneside Cinema.

It is hoped that the Tyneside Cinema will be a thriving focal point for cinema in the region, having initiated two new film festivals in 2003. It conducts outreach work and has an extremely strong educational programme. The Odeon name has returned to the city with its state-of-the-art multi-screen cinema complex inside the Gate in Newgate Street.

GALLOWGATE

As the name implies Gallowgate originally was a road that the condemned prisoners took on their journey to the gallows on the Town Moor from around 1480, and was not one of the original gates of the city walls. The name is actually a corruption of 'Gallows Gate'. Up to twenty thousand people would come to watch the occasion of an execution, either lining the streets or on the moor, with a great trade being done by the street hawkers and alehouses.

Over 40 people were executed between 1650 and 1829 on the gallows but in the eighteenth century a separate gallows was erected outside the Westgate purely for Northumberland criminals.

The road runs alongside the old city walls bordering St. Andrew's churchyard and at its west end has undergone massive redevelopment in the form of the Hanro Group Citygate Scheme. These three new impressive structures are built on the site of the old bus station, Rutherford College and the old Fever Hospital. During their construction houses were found that were even older than the medieval buildings that were expected to be revealed, necessitating a further archaeological excavation.

Constructed on the remains of the old city wall is a substantial building encompassing numbers 1-15 on the corner of Newgate Street and Gallowgate. Built in 1898-9 in the fashionable baroque style it has an eye-catching roofline with a green onion shaped copper dome and at the rear, overlooking St. Andrew's churchyard there is a line of dormer windows reminiscent of the town halls of the Netherlands.

On the north side of the street is Magnet House built in the early 1930s for the General Electric Company. Although not as blatantly Art Deco as its near neighbour the North East Co-op building in Newgate Street it does have a line of fascinating panels above the second floor windows that show the movement's influence, with each panel presenting a figure in stylised noble pose.

The Citygate development at Gallowgate

THE CITY WALLS

In 1265, it was decided to strengthen the defences of the town and castle by building a circular wall. When completed the walls extended for 3.2 kilometres around the town and were never less than 2 metres thick and up to 8 metres high.

The walls consisted of six main gateways called Sand Gate, West Gate, New Gate, Pandon Gate, Pilgrim Gate, and Close Gate along with seventeen towers and a number of smaller turrets built as lookout posts. Some of the towers had stone figures placed on them similar to those at Alnwick Castle today. Newgate, which had served as the prison of Newcastle, survived until a new castellated gaol was finished in 1823.

The route of the walls of Newcastle can still be traced today as some parts remain and the street pattern does indeed betray their course in places. Large sections were destroyed over the years but those parts that remain are still used for certain events and recitals.

Today the most impressive surviving section of the old town wall is to the west of the city centre off Chinatown's Stowell Street where four towers may be seen. This section has also retained its defensive ditch in front. A smaller section is also visible across the road in St. Andrew's churchyard.

It is possible to walk behind the street along the foot of the walls down to Blackfriars where you can get some idea of what they must have looked like and the part they have played in the city over the centuries.

The Morden Tower, for example, was partly rebuilt in 1770 and was used by the Company of Glaziers, Plumbers, Pewterers and Painters as a meeting place. Further along the Heber Tower still stands, used for a similar purpose by the armourers, curriers and feltmakers.

The building of the Central Station resulted in a long stretch of wall being demolished. However, a section still survives in Orchard Street to the south of the station where you can see how tall they were originally. The wall along the quayside was demolished as early as 1763.

The Pink and Gunner towers stood where Pink Lane runs today, the Carliol or Weavers Tower marked the northeastern corner of the wall and it was demolished in 1880. Some isolated towers do still exist in the city, one of these still stands in Tower Street and has a small gateway, called the Sally Port, from where defenders would sally forth against the enemy. On top of this tower is the Meeting Hall of the Shipwrights' Company built in 1716. On the eastern side of the tower above the cornice is a carved relief of a ship's hull. This proclaims who owned the building and explains why often the building was referred to as the Carpenters' Tower.

Another tower can be found in Croft Street. Known as Carliol Croft or the Plummer Tower it was used by the Cutler Company of the city for many years.

It is interesting to note that despite the need for defence in violent times the monks of Blackfriars were granted a small postern gate to give them access to their garden outside the walls! It is still visible today but now blocked up with stone.

The City Walls near Stowell Street

BLACKFRIARS

If you visit Blackfriars expecting to see a traditional medieval monastery you will be disappointed. What you will discover is a fascinating conglomeration of remains and outbuildings that have been modified and preserved by the city's guilds down the centuries.

Blackfriars was built by the Dominican order in the thirteenth and early fourteenth centuries. The Friary was arranged in the usual manner of the order's houses with the church and the everyday buildings clustered around a cloistered walk.

The Dominicans wore black habits, hence their name Blackfriars, as opposed to the Franciscans who wore grey and thus became known as the Greyfriars. The Dominicans were a preaching order and the friars here entertained the great and the good on many occasions.

During the Dissolution of the Monasteries in 1539, the friars were evicted and the property passed into hands of the Newcastle Corporation who leased it to nine of the craft guilds of the town as well as using it for almshouses. It is because of the long occupation by the guilds that so much of the Friary is preserved.

A restoration programme started in the late 1970s has included some meeting rooms and as a result, craft workshops and shops now also occupy the complex. Located in the twelfth century refectory, the Café Bar is an oasis for many city workers and it is said to be one of the oldest restaurant buildings in the country. The restored buildings are visible on three sides of the cloister with very informative display boards. The foundations of the church pillars can be seen, as they have been exposed and the area landscaped.

Great credit must be given to the designers of Jacobins Court that runs off Stowell Street into the north side of the Friary. The windows and arches are all pointed in a gothic style to complement the Friary and the wheat coloured bricks blend in perfectly. In short, it is a modern building that harmonises with its surroundings without sacrificing any of the needs of modern living.

A pleasant few hours can be spent walking around Blackfriars discovering the marks left by the monks and the guilds.

ST. ANDREW'S CHURCH

St. Andrew's Church is thought to be the oldest of the city's churches and is said to date from the middle of the twelfth century. When you open the door and walk inside through the Norman arches, the impression is more one of a small country church and this is reinforced on the outside with its leafy churchyard. Amongst the gravestones here is that of Charles Avison (1709-1770), the composer and organist, a plaque on the church wall in Newgate Street also commemorates him. He was organist at St. John's and later at St. Nicholas' Church. Of his many works, his anthem 'Sound the Loud Timbrel' is perhaps the best known.

The church is literally no more than a stone's throw from the city walls, a part of which still stand in its grounds and as a result, the building suffered from the besieging cannon during the Civil War siege. This is no surprise really, as the squat tower was used as a gun emplacement to cover this section of the walls so it must have attracted fire from the besiegers' cannon in the Castle Leazes. Inside the church, on a window ledge, cannonballs can still be seen with a note beside them saying 'A present from the Scot's Army'!

The medieval font cover is thought to be one of the finest in the country and no wonder when you look at the incredible carpentry that has gone into it. Adorned with delicate tracery and pinnacles it is some two metres tall and has a chain and pulley to lift it off the font.

St. Andrew's Street runs along the south side of the churchyard but was previously known as Darn Crook but the meaning of this name appears to have been lost. Most of the street was rebuilt in the early years of the twentieth century.

The section of the town walls at the end of the street has an overhanging walkway and the Andrew Tower once stood in the north-west section of the churchyard until being demolished along with part of the wall to give access to Gallowgate.

The old town walls inside the churchyard have interesting markings on them, which look like musical notes carved into the stones. Originally, they would have had a brass plate inside them and are thought to have been markers for the graves that butt up against the wall.

It is interesting that a practical use has been found for these old town walls, as they have been incorporated into a block of shops and offices which face onto Gallowgate, built about 1889.

Mr Scott, a lay preacher whose parish was St. Andrew's, invented a remedy for the digestion in 1903 and named it after his church! It is still well known today as Andrew's Liver Salts.
Mr Scott, with his partner Mr Turner, also invented Delrosa Rose Hip Syrup, which was intended to provide vitamin C for children whose diets had been deficient during the war.
Mr Turner and Mr Phillips then developed another well-known product, familiar to many, Milk of Magnesia.

Opposite: St Andrew's Church

CHINATOWN

Newcastle upon Tyne is a city full of surprises and in many ways Chinatown is a hidden gem, especially when you first discover its pagoda roofed telephone boxes. Until 1850, the street butted up against the town walls when a gap was made to link it with Bath Lane.

It is a wonder how anyone ever manages to park here, simply because, with its superb collection of authentic restaurants, Chinese supermarkets and shops, parking is always at a premium. Now Stowell Street is also used for access to the car park for The Gate complex on Newgate Street.

The Chinese community has done a remarkable job in preserving the buildings some of which date from 1824 (numbers 38-46 are the only survivors from the original terraces) and also encompass Edwardian, 1930s and post-war structures. This has been achieved by putting up fascinating shop fronts in a westernised Chinese style and leaving the floors above as they were originally constructed.

The arrival of the Chinese community in Newcastle upon Tyne can be traced back to the middle of the last century, far later than other major UK cities. The first Chinese restaurant in the city opened its doors in 1949 in Scotswood Road. Called the Marlbrough Café, it opened seven days a week from 10:00am to 11:00pm. A three-course lunch was available at a cost of a shilling and thruppence, which would be about six pence in today's coinage.

By the early 1960s the number of Chinese restaurants in Newcastle had grown to 15, however none

Chinese decorations in Stowell Street

of them were actually in Stowell Street, but it was to Stowell Street that The North East Chinese Association moved in 1983. Chinatown, as it is now, started to develop around the early 1980s and up to this time, Stowell Street was a run-down, unfashionable street. The first restaurant in the street was the Jade Garden, the Wing Hong supermarket and an arts and crafts shop above the Jade Garden opened at the same time.

Today Chinatown is no longer restricted to Stowell Street, spreading out to places such as Fenkle Street, beside Charlotte Square on the other side of Blackfriars. The Chinese influence has even spread to the Salvation Army Temple in Westgate Road, which has a sign with Chinese characters. During the Chinese New Year, there is the splendid spectacle of Chinese dragons and a festival atmosphere in Chinatown.

RICHARD GRAINGER

No city landscape is ever the result of the work of one individual. Over the years each city goes through a cycle of development and decay and the street plans and amenities improve or suffer accordingly. Some cities are the result, no matter what has influenced them since, of the vision of individuals. This is certainly true in Newcastle's case and the individual in point is Richard Grainger.

Born in High Friar Lane in 1797, Grainger, the son of a quayside porter, served his time as a carpenter and then as what we would call today a jobbing builder. His partnership with John Dobson and others would lead to the city becoming completely revitalised. He may not have had, as Augustus did of Rome, 'found it in brick and left it in marble' but he definitely took it away from a cramped timber base and gave it a visual power and grace of stone unrivalled anywhere else in the country.

In his early years, he built Higham Place during 1819-20 and worked on houses in the newly widened Blackett Street. In 1825, Grainger started work on Eldon Square using designs by John Dobson and by 1829, had begun another development, the superb Leazes Terrace, with Thomas Oliver as architect, surely the finest block of buildings in the city. Leazes Crescent and Leazes Place quickly followed, showing his great talent at aiming desirable buildings at all social classes and economic brackets. The splendid Royal Arcade completed in 1832 was Newcastle's first indoor shopping and commercial centre.

Grainger may have been astute in his marketing but he was also a smooth political operator. Hood Street, for example is named after the Lord Mayor of Newcastle at the time. His personality was such he could gain huge sums for his schemes and was quick enough to foresee problems before they arose, both with the construction and the personalities involved. At the age of 37 he commenced work on his great scheme for the centre of Newcastle and, remarkably, completed it within ten years. It was his vision that brought so much to the city; not only did he leave us great buildings but he had the foresight to build, with these buildings, the foundation stones for a thriving community with public houses, shops and music halls. Perhaps his greatest triumph is not just the Market that still bears his name but also the fact that we can walk down wide streets and see the sky above.

Leazes Terrace

GRAINGER MARKET

If you are walking around the city and worried about your weight you can always pop into the Grainger Market and weigh yourself! Originally, all covered markets had a weighing area for checking the goods being sold and the Grainger Market's weighing machine survives and is still well used today.

The Market is considered one of the sights of Newcastle upon Tyne with an atmosphere of its own. Traditionally, just about anything could be bought here and it still has a tremendous range of goods on sale. The oldest branch of Marks and Spencer in the country is here, trading in the Market since 1895 and still bearing the name Penny Bazaar.

Built in 1835 to house the traders displaced by Grainger's redevelopment of the city, the market eventually held around 150 butchers, 60 green-grocers and many other traders. Dobson's building, covering over 8,000 square metres, was at the time the most successful attempt at a traffic free shopping precinct in Newcastle.

When the building was opened, the corporation held two grand dinners inside the vegetable market, one at five shillings (25p) with wine included and the other at two shillings (10p) that included beer. It is said that touts were outside the market selling tickets for the meals at three times their face value.

This placing of the food distribution in one central place had an amazing effect on the city and Grainger, realising the business opportunities here, erected 12 public houses and a music hall close to the market. The music hall still stands in Nelson

The public weigh house, Grainger Market

Street with 'Music Hall' over the door and the date 1838, when it was built as the Gaiety Theatre. Charles Dickens appeared here for three nights in 1861 giving a selection of readings.

Someone else who saw the possibilities was Edward Muschamp Bainbridge who opened a draper shop near the market entrance. Bainbridge insisted on fixed prices and no bartering with only money changing hands and so it was not long before the shop had developed into one of the world's first department stores. By 1887, the store had more than 400 staff, vastly extending the range of goods sold. Photographs of the 1960s show the side entrance

from the Bigg Market with sunblinds drawn to protect the goods. This side entrance from one of Newcastle's busiest shopping areas on market days shows an interesting and very clever marketing strategy. Eventually the store moved to its present site in the Eldon Square Shopping Centre where it is now known as John Lewis.

The Grainger Market is still popular with the city's population, becoming almost a tradition for some. It is no wonder really that with its smells and hustle and bustle that it remains a vibrant part of Newcastle's life.

Marks & Spencer Penny Bazaar, Grainger Market

GRAINGER TOWN PROJECT

As far as unsung heroes go, the members of the Grainger Town Regeneration Project team and their successors are up there with the best of them. Without the dedication of this small band of people and the help they received from local authorities and businesses, Newcastle would still be the grubby city of the 1950s and 60s hiding its treasures under a layer of black dirt and grime.

Many people think of Grainger Town as the historic heart of Newcastle upon Tyne, which indeed it is. However, many of us think the term applies merely to the classical streets built by Richard Grainger in the 1830s and 1840s, whereas in fact it includes the thirteenth century Blackfriars and Stowell Street, the eighteenth century Westgate and the Bigg, Cloth and Groat markets. Amazingly about forty per cent of these buildings are listed as being of historical and architectural importance.

The area was not immune to the tidal wave of new centres of retail and commercial activity that eroded the economic base of so many cities in Britain in the 1980s and early 1990s, leaving properties to fall into disrepair. In 1992, this once prosperous area of Newcastle suddenly found itself with nearly one million square metres of unoccupied floor space and with a falling residential population. The once beautifully coloured buildings were blackened with car exhaust fumes and other polluting materials.

This meant that any potential investors or businesses were not attracted to the area, so rapid action was needed. The Grainger Town Project was established in 1997 in partnership with Newcastle City Council, English Partnership and English Heritage with the aim of reversing this trend.

Since the project started, great strides have been made in regenerating the area, improving the environment and revitalising business, social and cultural life. This manifests itself in not only the improved pavements and walkways but also in the people of Newcastle's increased pride and pleasure for this area. This in turn appears to be leading to the birth of a café culture in the streets with people strolling around appreciating the value and beauty of the architecture.

The ethos of high quality that underpinned the entire project's activities. The use of high quality Caithness stone and granite encouraged the introduction of bespoke granite, glass and stainless steel street furniture and the introduction of public art helped to generate confidence.

During the project's lifetime, 277 businesses were set up, 1,500 jobs and 500 homes were created or planned, historic buildings were rescued and pedestrianisation schemes removed much of the traffic congestion.

On 31st March 2003, the project closed down having achieved and indeed exceeded, its objectives. A key success factor was the Grainger Town Partnership itself, with agencies and individuals working together towards a common purpose with a particularly strong partnership developing between the project and the private sector. The project was all about restoring heritage buildings and bringing them back into economic use in a way that was sympathetic to their fine architectural quality.

Street sign, Grainger Town

A number of schemes continues including the creative lighting scheme. Responsibility for the future maintenance and improvement of the area and on-going schemes has been transferred to the City Centre Panel, supported by the City Centre Development Team.

Opposite: Grainger Market

BETWEEN THE WARS

Between the First and Second World Wars, the predominant look of architecture for civil and other grand buildings in Newcastle was the Art Deco style.

It could be argued that the North Eastern Co-op Stores building in Newgate Street is the most impressive survivor of the 1930s left in the city; there are certainly very few buildings that have a public barometer on the exterior!

The roof of the building is incredibly detailed with green glazed tiles and its two towers are topped off with a shimmering green mosaic and decorative metalwork. What really sets off the building, as an art deco structure, is the interior staircases of the towers with their marble cladding and steel handrails supported by the small metal figures straining to hold the rail up. The pillars on the ground floor seem like stylised lotus flowers with rectangular petals of green, white and brown.

Another survivor from the 1930s is Pilgrim Street's Art Deco Paramount Cinema. It was taken over by Odeon in the 1960s and despite being the most complete of the UK's six provincial Paramount theatres, it is no longer a listed building.

As well as showing the top films of the day, it had a huge Wurlitzer organ, an orchestra, and a troupe of dancing girls. Unfortunately this building now faces an uncertain future.

Further along Pilgrim Street on the corner of Market Street is Carliol House, built in 1927. Many consider this to be one of the best inter-war buildings in Newcastle. Clad in Portland stone and built in classical proportions this is a very impressive building which was constructed for the North Eastern Electric Supply Company.

The Central Police Station, built in 1931, is also built out of Portland Stone with a huge doorway and an enormous single window flanked by columns above it. These columns stretch along Pilgrim Street and Market Street giving a true sense of grandeur.

Other buildings sprang up in this period, some were built at Woolsington to the north-west of the city in 1935. One of the buildings and the small huts that stood beside it marked the beginnings of the Newcastle International Airport terminal we know today.

In 1919, R.G. Roberts was appointed City Housing Architect and by 1935, he and his team had built 11,000 new houses. Many of these were in estates of semi-detached, two storey dwellings with gardens. Roberts was appointed the first official City Architect in 1936.

There was also a lively theatre scene and literary circle in the city at this time, attracting names such as W.H. Auden and A.J. Cronin. The famous broadcaster and writer Nancy Spain spent her youth in Tankerville Place, Jesmond and her detective novel 'Cinderella Goes to the Morgue' is set in a pantomime at the Theatre Royal.

 From September 1763, streets within the city walls were lit by public oil lamps. It was not until 1812 that street lighting was extended into the suburbs.
Mains electricity was not available in Newcastle until 1890.

Opposite: Magnet House, Gallowgate

LET THERE BE LIGHT

Street furniture, Grey Street

The urban renaissance that Newcastle upon Tyne has undergone in recent years has spawned another aspect of the city's character. Newcastle has always had the reputation of being a party city at night, but now with the regeneration of Grainger Town, a different form of nightlife is emerging and, what is more, is spreading outwards away from the city's core to areas such as Jesmond.

More and more a 'strolling, café lifestyle' is emerging in the city after dark. Perhaps more reminiscent of the warm climes of the Mediterranean than the cool air of the Tyne Valley, the fact that this night culture is developing is due in part to the changes made to the city's lighting. Newcastle City Council has spent a lot of time and effort in recent years planning how Newcastle could look at night. As a result of this Newcastle has become one of the most beautifully illuminated cities in the country.

Streets, buildings and memorials have been enhanced at night by lighting, especially now the beautiful stonework has been cleaned and the natural colours exposed. One classic example of this is the Theatre Royal visible up and down Grey Street. Small features have been deliberately included into the fabric of the city to add another dimension to the ground level after dark. A prime example of this are head cubes laid flush in the plinth of Grey's Monument. Virtually unnoticeable by day, at night they shine upwards in a soft hue. Designed by Simon Watkinson in 2002, they are images of the statue's head looked at from different angles taken from a cast of the head when it was being cleaned, then cut from perspex to achieve the desired result.

People need to sit down and chat, to rest and just watch the world go by and throughout the Grainger Town is a series of benches, some of which have etched glass forming a back to rest against. During the day, these benches serve the same purpose for weary shoppers but at night, the designs in the glass are illuminated by LEDs making a cool blue addition to the other-wise dominant yellows and oranges of the street lighting. The result of work by Cate Watkinson and Julia Darling in 2001, the benches are not only a subtle and almost witty addition to the areas visual landscape, they are also superbly practical.

Other light sculptures keep appearing, some, although totally modern in their concept, hark back to a gentler time, such as the red and blue neon lit clocks and barometer of the Co-op building in Newgate Street. Once again here is a link with the past and present as neon is used in the 'Full Circle' found on the front of Nexus House on the corner of St. James' Boulevard and Westgate Road.

Designed by Ron Hasleden in 2002 the sculpture, 11 metres in diameter, is made up of two concentric rings of white and yellow neon. Although fixed in position the circle gives the illusion of altering in shape as you walk along St. James' Boulevard. An illusion no doubt enhanced for some of those walking homewards from a good night out!

Opposite: Celebrating the New Year on Newcastle Quayside

NORTHUMBERLAND STREET

Mention Northumberland Street and it's a fair possibility that you will also think of Fenwick. J.J. Fenwick opened his shop in 1882, in the exclusive residential Northumberland Street. The shop moved to its present site three years later and by 1914 employed 400 people. It was J.J. Fenwick's son Fred who transformed the shop into a Parisian style walk-round *grand magasin*. The new style store dramatically improved the flow of customers from around 295 per day in 1905 to nearly three thousand per day.

The growth of retailing in Newcastle received a substantial boost with the arrival of the electric tram in 1901. Bainbridge claimed that the incredible number of 2,500 trams passed their store each day. However, it was the arrival of C&A Modes and Marks and Spencer in 1932 which along with Fenwick helped to establish Northumberland Street as the premier shopping street in the city. Today retailing in Newcastle is dominated by the massively enlarged Fenwick store, the modern Eldon Square shopping mall and Marks and Spencer.

Eventually the traffic in Northumberland Street became so busy that a footbridge was necessary to get from one side to the other. During the 1990s, Northumberland Street was paved and pedestrianised and now shoppers can go about their business in safety, with less noise and free from traffic fumes. No trace now remains of the lines used by the horse-drawn trams that once ran up this street towards Barras Bridge until the 1930s when the motor buses and trolley buses began to replace these trams. At one point, the city had over 64 kilometres of tramlines running across it, the last trolley bus ran in 1966.

Northumberland Street

Not much remains to show that the street was first built as an upmarket eighteenth century residential area. Northumberland Street probably had the city's first domestic classical building at numbers 37-39, built in 1832 and designed by Thomas Oliver, who also designed Leazes Terrace.

By looking up as you walk down the street, you can find some amazing sights. Just to the south of the Eldon Square Shopping Centre entrance are some wonderful first floor stained glass windows. They both depict larger than life women dressed in Tudor costume, one with the word 'cutlery' and one with 'clocks', giving some idea what the shop once was.

Another fascinating building is halfway down the street on the west side, originally built as a store for Boots & Co. around 1900. It has an amazing top two stories. Apart from the windows and the classical stonework it has four figures, each set in its own niche: Harry Hotspur, Thomas Bewick, Sir John Marley and Richard Thornton, all associated with the city's history and looking down upon the crowds below.

In 1783, street names were put up for the first time in Newcastle. Horse-drawn trams were introduced in 1879 and survived until April 13th 1901. The new electric trams began operating on 16th December 1901.

Horse-drawn cabs made a brief reappearance in September 1942 due to a petrol shortage.

In 1908, there were only 251 motor vehicles in Newcastle.

According to police records there were no more than 347 registered cars, 813 motorcycles and 44 licensed taxis in Newcastle in 1914.

Four figures associated with Newcastle's history adorn this building in Northumberland Street

LAING ART GALLERY

It is difficult to decide in what light the 'Blue Carpet' outside the Laing Art Gallery should be viewed. On bright days, the sun catches the grains in the pavement and sets them sparkling. The purpose-made tiles are made of a durable white resin mixed with recycled glass shards. After dark, the underground lights set in the pavement below the twisting seats also give an interesting slant to the city's nightlife. Bollards prevent traffic entering the area, so creating both a secure space for pedestrians and a stage for plays and performances.

In addition to its permanent collection, the Laing runs a continuous and lively programme of exhibitions all year round and has an annual touring partnership with the National Gallery in London, helping to bring work from its collection to the region. Housed in a listed Edwardian baroque building the gallery is one of the North East's premier art venues. A point exemplified by the frieze of carved figures symbolising 'The Arts' set beneath the dome.

The Laing commissions work by leading contemporary artists as well as running an extensive and popular outreach programme for the local community, including weekly lectures taking place each week that are open to all. Local schools and colleges are not forgotten, as the gallery holds educational events aimed at developing the artistic awareness of young people and its Children's Gallery is immensely popular.

Inside the building you will find a large and impressive collection of stunning watercolours, pottery,

silver, local glassware and British oil paintings. In particular, the gallery has an excellent representative collection of Victorian paintings, including works by members of the Pre-Raphaelite Brotherhood.

The paintings in the Barbour Watercolour Gallery are changed regularly to show the extent of the 4,000 watercolours and drawings that are held in the collection which includes works by artists such as Gainsborough, Turner and local artist Ralph Hedley.

John Martin's work is also held in the Laing. He was born in 1789 and after being apprenticed to a coach painter in Newcastle, moved to London in 1806, and by 1811 he was exhibiting at the Royal Academy. His grandiose biblical scenes caught the popular imagination and his painting 'Belshazzar's Feast' made him famous. An engraving of this painting adorned the Brontes' parlour wall at Howarth. He is sometimes mistakenly referred to as 'Mad Martin', possibly through confusion with his brother Jonathan, who tried to set fire to York Minster.

Opened in 1904, the Laing Gallery was a gift to his adopted city from Alexander Laing, a wealthy wine merchant, to commemorate his successful fifty-year business career. The Laing Art Gallery was originally an addition to the Central Public Library. Unfortunately, only the gallery now remains as the library was demolished in 1969 to make way for John Dobson Street. One hundred years later, it was completely refurbished, thanks to generous donations from local companies and organisations that recognised its continuing importance to the life of the city and its inhabitants.

Laing Art Gallery interior

SQUARES

As the city developed in the late eighteenth century, new fashionable streets were laid out for the increasingly affluent population. It is something of a surprise that this was the trend in Newcastle and that the city did not emulate the leafy squares of the capital or the crescents of Bath and Edinburgh. In fact Leazes Terrace could be described as a square turned inside out.

The nearest the city has to that style of living is Charlotte Square, named after the wife of George III and built in 1769 by William Newton as speculative property development. Like the larger squares in London, the garden in the centre was strictly reserved for the use of the residents.

The city's best known square, Eldon Square, gave its name to both the Eldon Square Shopping Centre and to Eldon Gardens. It is named after John Scott, Lord Eldon, Lord Chancellor of England who is best remembered in his native city for eloping with Bessie Surtees from her father's house in Sandhill.

The oldest of the city's squares, Carliol Square, like Charlotte Square, lies within the perimeter of the town walls and is named after the prominent medieval family the Carliols, who held the offices of Mayor and Bailiff during the Medieval period. One of their number, Henry, was Mayor for ten years in succession from 1254 and another, who was Mayor five times, succeeded him. They also gave their name to Carliol Croft, an open space by Carliol Tower inside the walls where some of the trade guilds would meet on Corpus Christi day to perform their miracle plays.

Carliol Square was the site of the new prison built by John Dobson in 1823 to replace the town gaol that had been in Newgate since the Middle Ages. The prison was in

Central Square artwork, 'Reaching for the Stars'

use until 1925 when it was demolished. In 1931 the city's telephone exchange was moved to a new building in Carliol Square from the site of the General Post Office in St. Nicholas' Square.

Hanover Square once held one of the country's most important Nonconformist chapels, built in 1727 with seating for 600 people. Many of the city's elite were members of the congregation and the Rev. William Turner was minister here in 1782.

Behind Central Station is a huge bronze statue of an arm with an open palm facing upwards. This sculpture is called 'Reaching for the Stars' and stands in a lane in Central Square. Designed by Carey Jones architects, Central Square is the latest of the city's squares and won a national award for creating prime office space from the former Royal Mail sorting office.

On the morning of 22nd September 1761, Newcastle awoke to peals of bells and the firing of guns and this was repeated every three hours throughout the day to celebrate the coronation of Their Majesties King George III and Queen Charlotte.
In the evening, Newcastle was splendidly illuminated, with houses, churches, offices, public buildings and water fountains all bedecked with as many candles as possible. Even the ship 'Royal Oak' had 200 lamps suspended from her rigging and the corporation of Newcastle hosted a magnificent concert and ball.
What a sight all this must have been!
Sir Walter Blackett did not want anyone to miss out on the celebrations so he had £50 distributed to the poor inhabitants and the prisoners in the gaol.

CIVIC CENTRE

The Civic Centre stands next to the Church of St. Thomas the Martyr in the Haymarket and when viewed through the trees of the churchyard, this impressive municipal government building of Scandinavian style, blends in well with the surrounding mix of old and new buildings.

This modern complex serves the city in much the same way as the buildings of Blackfriars did in previous centuries. Set in the middle is the Garth, a quadrangle of lawns and seats, giving the feeling of a twentieth century cloister walk, an impression enhanced by the cloister like arches on the West Side. The grooved drum shaped council chamber, which could easily be taken for the modern equivalent of a medieval chapter house, stands raised up on piers forming a spectacular ceremonial entrance.

Newcastle's old Town Hall used to stand in the Bigg Market. However, the Council anticipated the need to construct a new, larger building to cater for the needs of the city's expanding post-war population. The tall white office blocks and mushroom capped round chamber were designed by the City Architect, George Kenyon and constructed between 1958 and 1969.

The Civic Centre Tower is capped by a beacon decorated with three castles taken from the city's coat of arms and on the lantern are twelve cast bronze stylised heads of seahorses. The heads are 1.4 metres high and 1.6 metres wide and are there because the seahorse forms part of the city's crest. Here also is the carillon, one of only fourteen in the country, which has been rung by Dr. Ian Brunt most Saturdays since 1990.

In the open square in the middle of the Civic Centre is a piece of beautiful bronze sculpture depicting swans soaring

into flight, a stunning work by David Wynne. They represent the City's links with the countries of Scandinavia, links reinforced by the fact that King Olaf of Norway officially opened the Civic Centre in 1968. Every Christmas, Newcastle receives a Christmas tree from the people of Bergen and it is displayed in front of the Civic Centre.

Another magnificent work of art can be seen on the round chamber where 5 metres up on the exterior wall is David Wynne's sandstone statue of River-God with water pouring from his outstretched hand.

Whatever else it does, the Civic Centre makes a grand statement with its 1960s architecture being complemented by the thoughtful use of modern art. Since completion in 1969, the building has had time to mellow and in a city where the presence of 1960s architecture is often viewed with mixed feelings, Newcastle's Civic Centre is often looked upon with pride and affection.

Between 1920 and 1939 the corporation built 11,336 houses and 1,353 flats.
The estimated population of Newcastle upon Tyne has increased from around 850 in 1100 to over a quarter of a million by the 21st century.

Year	Estimated population
1100	800 to 900
1770	24,000
1871	128,443
1939	291,300
1981	203,591
2001	259,536

David Wynne's sculpture River-God Tyne, Newcastle Civic Centre

HAYMARKET

The triangular space at the junction of Percy Street and Northumberland Street was once a dirty trackway covered with ruts and puddles of foul water. Because it was so bad, it was paved over in 1809 and became the Parade Ground, where the local militia and volunteers were inspected. Its present name dates back to 1824 when the city's hay market was set up here and held every Tuesday.

The Haymarket is dominated by the red and green turreted old Newcastle Breweries building and the South African War Memorial, which was unveiled in 1908, designed by Eyre Macklin, and commemorates the men of the Northumbrian regiments who fell in the Boer War between 1899 and 1902.

Nowadays the Haymarket is a bustling and diverse area with its bookshops, galleries, bus and Metro stations and the entrance to Northumberland Street. It is also the heart of the student district, with the nearby City Hall being a popular music venue. The academic bookshop, Blackwell's, was the Grand Hotel from 1890 until 1958, when it was purchased by the University of Newcastle and used as a senior common room until 1983.

The Newcastle Playhouse (Northern Stage) at Barras Bridge also contributes to the city's culture by staging international productions. Previously the Palace Theatre, built in the closing years of the nineteenth century, carried out this function but the theatre was demolished in 1961. Eventually temporary shops were erected on the site and are still there today. The Hotspur Public House was close

to the stage door and many a famous thespian dropped in there for a stiffener before treading the boards.

To the north is the Church of St. Thomas the Martyr, standing by the Civic Centre on Barras Bridge. Built by John Dobson during the period 1827-1830 it was the first church in Newcastle built in the Gothic revival style and stands on the site of the former St. Mary Magdalene's Hospital. By the west door of the church stands a memorial to the men of the Royal Tank Regiment, whilst to the north is a memorial to the men of the Northumberland Fusiliers. During the First World War, the city recruited the Tyneside Irish and the Tyneside Scottish Brigades into the regiment.

Dobson also designed the adjacent St. Mary's Place, looking for the entire world like a neo-Tudor terrace. Many of the houses now have shopfronts but some have preserved the original doorways with iron railings flanking the steps.

Barras Bridge crossed the deep dene of the Bailiff Burn that later in its course turned into the Pandon Burn and entered the Tyne at Pandon. In 1819, the bridge had to be rebuilt, as it was too narrow for the increased traffic of the Great North Road, which entered the city at this point. The dene was filled up in 1835 when the bridge and the mill that stood beside it were demolished.

The Haymarket Metro Station fits neatly into this landscape and evidence of travellers of an earlier age can be found diagonally opposite. Here are the

St Thomas' Church, Haymarket

imposing buildings of the Grand Hotel and the Crows' Nest Hotel, a smaller baroque building with its name still visible above the doors. Both of these names signify a change in fashion from the names of the old coaching inns, which were being demolished in the name of progress. These hotels were the first port of call for anyone entering the city by the Great North Road.

St Thomas' Church, Haymarket and Barras Bridge

METRO SYSTEM

Many times in a city's existence, something comes along to change dramatically the way its inhabitants live and to improve their quality of life. In Newcastle, the work of Grainger and Dobson is one example but the most recent improvement has been the introduction of the Metro system.

The Metro was the country's first light rapid transit system and it has completely altered the life of the city. Used not only by commuters, the system also provides great recreational opportunities by allowing people to visit the coast at such places as Whitley Bay and Tynemouth as well as to go shopping or for a night out in Sunderland or Newcastle. Others use the system to visit the countryside, to places like The Great North Forest or to take the direct link to Newcastle International Airport for business or holiday flights.

In 1974, the first civil engineering contracts were let for the construction of tunnels under Newcastle and Gateshead central areas. Ground conditions under Newcastle were favourable for tunnelling, as some sections being driven mainly through boulder clay.

The Metro has a total route length of around 76 kilometres, with almost seventy-five per cent being converted British Rail line. There are 58 Metro stations, all unmanned, ranging from large underground stations in the centres of Newcastle and Gateshead, to small wayside halts in outlying areas.

The hub of the Metro is the interchange at Monument, where north, south, and east-west lines intersect, whilst the overall control room is based at South Gosforth with links to five local authority control rooms. The high degree of automation and low manning levels on the system have made the Tyne and Wear Metro one of the most cost-effective metropolitan railways in the world.

As time has progressed, the public service offered by the system has expanded. Now works of art can be seen as you travel around and a series of booklets set out guided walks for all the family, beginning and ending at metro stations. Being able to park cars at the stations and enter the city by Metro has also helped to relieve traffic congestion.

The face of the city has been affected by the Metro system. Mounted on high poles, for easy recognition, large yellow cubes with a black 'M' are dotted around the city, whilst the architecture of the stations, such as the Haymarket, adds another dimension to the face of Newcastle. The river vista too has benefited by the building of the Queen Elizabeth II Bridge across the Tyne.

In recent years, the Metro has been upgraded, resulting in numerous improvements including, refurbished trains with more room for wheelchairs and buggies and better seating. Many of the system's stations now have real-time platform indicators, help points, CCTV cameras, payphones, lifts and escalators.

With 40 million journeys a year being made on the Metro it is a sharp contrast to the days when eighteenth century travellers gathered in the yards of

The familiar Metro symbol

the Queen's Head, the Turk's Head and the Half Moon and other inns waiting for the horse-drawn coaches with names such as the High Flyer, the Telegraph and the Royal Mail.

The first electric tram ran from New Bridge Street to Benton on March 29th 1904 amid great celebration. This was followed by staged electrification of a complete loop from Tynemouth to Newcastle Central Station.
Electric trains served the area well for six decades, eventually evolving into today's Tyne and Wear Metro system.

The Metro Station at South Gosforth

UNIVERSITY OF
NEWCASTLE UPON TYNE

Newcastle is considered one of the oldest university towns in England. With over 16,000 students, the University of Newcastle is the only one where teaching began in the faculty of medicine, with the first formal lecture given in 1832 in Bell's Court.

The university first appeared on the Barras Bridge site in 1888 when the College of Physical Science moved from Westgate Road to a new building on Lax's Gardens. The College of Medicine moved to the Haymarket site in 1937 to be joined by Armstrong College. These two colleges united to become King's College under the auspices of the Federal University of Durham. It was not until 1963, when the Federal University dissolved, that King's College became the University of Newcastle upon Tyne.

Still centred on the majestic brick tower of the Armstrong College buildings the university has developed into a thriving contemporary university campus, on a site of over 18 hectares, close to the centre of the city near the Haymarket. It has become a city within a city and there is no doubt that it contributes immensely to the cultural and entertainment life of Newcastle. A vigorous building programme over the past 30 years has created many other additions to the campus so that the original buildings are now almost obscured by the new ones.

The University houses the Hatton Gallery, named after Professor R. G. Hatton, Armstrong College's first Professor of Fine Art. This gallery is renowned for its permanent collections, including the Fred and Dianna Uhlman African Collection and has a regular programme of touring exhibitions.

Just inside the Quadrangle is the Museum of Antiquities which specialises in the archaeology of the north-east of England and contains a very fine 12 metre long model of Hadrian's Wall. The Shefton Museum of Greek Art and Archaeology houses Celtic, Roman and Near Eastern items.

A few steps up Kings Walk from the Haymarket are the Grand Assembly Rooms with what Pevsner referred to as 'a jolly overdecorated façade'. Built in 1889 these rooms served as a British Restaurant during World War II before eventually becoming one of the University's Sports Centres.

Further along is the Union building, home of the Students' Union which provides all the necessary support services and houses the many student societies including Student Community Action Newcastle (SCAN), which provides volunteers for local projects as well as initiating some of its own. A registered charity, it helps over 500 students each year to be involved in the local community.

This rather attractive building was built in 1924 in the neo-Jacobean style and designed by a local firm of architects, Robert Burns Dick, who also designed the Laing Art Gallery.

The university is involved in the administration and running of the Hancock Museum and has recently put forward a very ambitious plan to construct a

'The Arches' at The University of Newcastle

Combined Museum which would incorporate all the university's museums on one site, eventually forming part of a 'Cultural Quarter' on the campus.

The University of Newcastle is now seeing the fruition of its plans to become a world-class research-intensive university and is committed to deliver teaching of the highest quality. With ever widening horizons, combined with superb facilities the popularity of the university continues to increase, attracting more home and overseas students than ever before.

The King's Hall, University of Newcastle

UNIVERSITY OF NORTHUMBRIA AT NEWCASTLE

The University of Northumbria is in the heart of the city and only a few minutes walk from the Haymarket. It was first established as a polytechnic in 1969 and inaugurated as a university on 1st September 1992. The largely modularized curriculum is delivered to just over 25,000 students, about 16,000 of whom are full-time. Although not its official name it is known as Northumbria University and has quickly become one of the UK's leading modern universities.

Newcastle Polytechnic was formed in 1969 from the amalgamation of the College of Art & Industrial Design, the Municipal College of Commerce, and Rutherford College of Technology with roots dating as far back as the nineteenth century. Friends and colleagues of Dr. Rutherford, the evangelist and pioneer of free secondary and technical education, opened Rutherford College in 1894, four years after his death, as a memorial to his work for education in Newcastle.

The City College of Education became part of the Polytechnic in 1974 and the Northern Counties College of Education joined in 1976, making the institution a major teacher-training centre. The Bede, Newcastle and Northumbria College of Health Studies merged with the University in 1995 and consolidated Northumbria's position as one of the largest universities in the country.

The Newcastle City campus houses the administration centre, the library, the Students' Union Centre, Student Services and most of the teaching accommodation. There is another campus a few miles out of town at Coach Lane that used to be the Northern Counties Teacher Training College and here learning and teaching facilities are provided for around 5,000 students on courses related to education, health and social work. The buildings on this new 11 hectare site blend in well with the open space environment, complemented by attractive landscaping. The Business School at Longhurst Hall, an eighteenth century country mansion, provides a high quality centre for postgraduate education.

The city campus has a mixture of building styles, from the Victorian Sutherland Building, through to the 1960s Wynne-Jones Centre. The entire south facing façade of the Northumberland building has been clad with solar panels, which are intended to provide a significant proportion of the building's power needs.

The university has refurbished a variety of old buildings near the city campus, including student accommodation at Garth Heads, Art Conservation housed in Burt Hall, Information Technology and teaching facilities in the Trinity Building, a deconsecrated church, and the Drill Hall. The Law School is housed in the old Dental School and Hospital, a nineteenth century building now renamed the Sutherland Building. Sir Arthur Sutherland provided £50,000 towards the cost of the extensive alterations to convert the old Medical

University of Northumbria at Newcastle

College into the Dental School and Hospital, which was opened here in 1948.

Northumbria University has developed close links with the local and regional community and strives not only to make the university accessible, but to strengthen the economic, environmental, and cultural life of the region. The University Gallery is well known for presenting a varied programme of touring and temporary exhibitions covering art and photography.

HANCOCK MUSEUM

Over 100,000 people visit the Hancock Museum every year giving it the enviable distinction that only a minority of the population of Newcastle have not passed through its doors. The Hancock has been successful with its interactive exhibitions and displays, especially with its famous dinosaur events that attract people of all ages to the museum, and with workshops, activities, and outreach.

The Hancock Museum's origins can be traced to about 1780, when Marmaduke Tunstall began collecting ethnographic and natural history material from all over the world. After Tunstall's death, his collection was purchased in 1791, by George Allan of Darlington. In 1793, when the Literary and Philosophical Society of Newcastle was founded, its activities included the formation of a small museum and they acquired Allan's collection in 1823.

The Natural History Society of Northumberland, Durham, and Newcastle upon Tyne (now the Natural History Society of Northumbria) was founded in 1829 as an offshoot of the Literary and Philosophical Society. The museum's collections soon outgrew this building and the new Newcastle Museum was opened on its present site in 1884. The museum was renamed the Hancock Museum in honour of John and Albany Hancock, two local naturalists who had been so instrumental in its formation.

Interestingly enough, less than 3% of the museum's collections of over 600,000 objects are on display and a walk around behind the scenes is even more fascinating. Here, the original beautiful wooden display cupboards and cases still hold their

The Hancock Museum

contents, as they did for their pioneering owners in the eighteenth and nineteenth centuries.

The Hancock collections are designated as an internationally important scientific resource. Over the years many other collections have been absorbed into the museum. These collections continue to be actively used by researchers from all over the world. There is research material of international significance within the collections and these provide an irreplaceable resource for the students of the city's universities and colleges to assist them with

their studies.

Outside the museum is Sir Hamo Thornycroft's bronze statue of Lord Armstrong of Cragside, a generous benefactor to the Natural History Society. Some one hundred metres up Claremont Road, cut into the banks, is a steel door that was the entrance to an air raid shelter beneath the museum during the Second World War. This is the midway point of Victoria Tunnel that runs from Spital Tongues Colliery down to the Ouseburn.

Opposite: Sutherland Building, University of Northumbria at Newcastle

VICTORIA TUNNEL

Like other major cities, Newcastle has many tunnels under its streets; most are concerned with sewage and drains but there are others of a very different nature.

One of the longest and least known about is the Victoria Tunnel, a 1840s waggonway that runs for just over 3 kilometres from Spital Tongues to the Lower Ouseburn valley. It was built to carry coal from the Spital Tongues' Colliery down to the mouth of the Ouseburn, all set to be loaded straight on to colliers ready for export.

At its deepest the tunnel is some twenty-four metres underground with the fall from the colliery to the river being seventy-three metres. This fall allowed the tunnel to use gravity for the trucks bearing the coal to the staithes on Tyne Street near the present Glasshouse Bridge. For the return journey, the empty trucks were pulled back up the tunnel by a stationary 40-horsepower engine at the colliery.

Originally known as The Spital Tongues Colliery Tunnel, its construction began in June 1839 with the tunnel being dug through boulder clay and taking two and a half years to complete, with the brick and stone lining carried out by David Nixon, a local builder from Prudhoe Street. On the tunnel's completion the 200 workmen were treated to a substantial supper and strong ale by Mrs Dixon, hostess of the Unicorn Inn in the Bigg market. The tunnel fell into disuse when the colliery finally closed in 1860.

During the Second World War, parts of the tunnel

The Victoria Tunnel

were opened up as an air raid shelter and entrances can still be seen in the grass bank beneath the Hancock Museum in Claremont Road and in Ouse Street.

With the help of English Heritage and Newcastle City Council, the Ouseburn Trust has undertaken a series of repairs and improvements to the tunnel and school parties and other groups frequently access the tunnel through the entrance in Ouse Street for educational visits.

During an air raid in the evening of December 29th 1941, ten bombs are recorded as having fallen on Holderness Road, Byker and the Matthew Bank area, killing nine people and seriously injuring sixteen, with sixty-four slightly injured.

LEAZES

The Leazes conjures up a vision of open space used today by the people of Newcastle for walks and picnics. Castle Leazes and Leazes Park with its bowling green and boating lake provide a green lung for the city. Generations of students have walked across the Leazes on their way to the Halls of Residence from the university.

Leazes Park was the first area laid out for recreation in the city and was opened in 1873. This came about as a direct result of 3,000 working men petitioning Newcastle Council for 'ready access to some open ground for the purpose of health and recreation'.

Much to the delight of those who have grown up in the area, the authorities have refurbished the park to its original glory. Amongst the exciting things to happen is the reintroduction of the two major gateways, including the Jubilee Gates installed to commemorate the 60th year of Queen Victoria's reign, the bandstand and 950 metres of cast iron railings. Despite several threats to its existence, the park's future has been assured, due to the support of the people of Newcastle, who will be able to continue to use the park now and in the future.

However, the name also refers to other important parts of the city's development, some still present and some that have vanished into the mists of time. Take the Leazes Arcade, for instance, which once flourished nearby. The building still has the large gold letters on its north end announcing the arcade's presence to entice customers in, whilst at the bottom of Leazes Park Lane, at its junction with Percy Street, one building has simply stunning bow windows in its southern end.

Tradition has it that it was King John who granted the Leazes to several Burgesses of Newcastle to recompense them for the loss of property they sustained when he created the moat around the castle.

Leazes Terrace was designed by Thomas Oliver, an apprentice of John Dobson, and built by Grainger (1829-34) in the Palladian style. On seeing it for the first time, you would be excused for using every superlative you can think of. Restored by the University of Newcastle, the honey-coloured stone is one of the joys of the city in the evening light. The trees of the park at the northern end lend a further air of calm and beauty to these lovely buildings. Unfortunately, today the football stadium of St. James' Park dramatically overshadows them but one can still imagine their imposing stately elegance when they were first built.

Nearby is the delightful Leazes Crescent, which, though not on such a grand scale, still evokes the atmosphere of the period.

Leazes Park and Leazes Terrace

ST JAMES' PARK

The history of St James' Park is forever connected with the Leazes, as it was from an affluent resident of Leazes Terrace who entitled Newcastle West End Cricket Club to play on the land in the 1880s.

The West End club started a football team and at the other end of the city the Newcastle East End Cricket club followed suit. The pitch at this time was situated close to the actual site of the city's gallows and had quite a drop towards the present Gallowgate end.

The two clubs amalgamated in 1892 with a match against Middlesborough, and it was also in that year that the black and white stripes were first worn. Ratification by the F.A. was granted in 1895, with the first changing rooms situated in the Lord Hill public house on Barrack Road.

In the late twentieth century the stadium renewed the contact with the Leazes when Sir John Hall, at the time chairman of the club, unsuccessfully put forward plans for a new stadium on the Town Moor and Leazes Park.

The St James' Park ground had a £70 million reconstruction carried out during the 1990s increasing its capacity to 52,000. Today, like all football stadiums, it carries out a mutli-purpose role, hosting many events and exhibitions, from wedding receptions to business meetings.

St. James' Park, Newcastle United FC

The player with the most League and Cup appearances in a career was Jimmy Lawrence with 496 appearances (1904-22).

Record attendance at St James' Park is 68,386 at the match v Chelsea in September, 1930.

Record victory stands at 13-0 at the match v Newport County in October, 1946.

TOWN MOOR AND THE HOPPINGS

Town Moor is one of the features that make the city so special, with around 400 hectares of open space offering the city a green heart, with the Freemen of the City still retaining the right to graze their cattle here. Its own Act of Parliament governs its land tenure and use and the Moor is the location for the annual visit of the Hoppings, Europe's largest travelling fair.

In the eighteenth century, horse racing began to take place on the Moor and from 1715, a 'race week' was held. This eventually evolved into a huge festival of summer activities including cockfighting, sideshows, beer tents, stalls and entertainments. So popular did the horse racing become that in 1800, a grandstand was erected. The Grandstand Committee bought the old Brandling estate at Gosforth and moved there in 1880 to set up a permanent racecourse. From 1904, a tramline ran to the gates to accommodate the race-goers.

Newcastle's Town Moor was the meeting place for supporters of political causes and between seventy and a hundred thousand Chartists met there in May 1839. The Moor was also the sporting centre for the miners of the south Northumberland coalfield. In particular, 'potshare' bowling, a form of road bowling, similar to the French game of boules, was still played in the first decade of the twentieth century and it was very popular with the pitmen. The bowls were extremely heavy and a course of 240 metres was laid out on the eastern edge of the Moor. The fight against the demon drink manifested itself in many ways in the city but the largest of these was the Temperance Fair held on the Moor, which became the forerunner of the Hoppings.

The Hoppings attracts tens of thousands of visitors to the Moor in the last week of June each year. It was said that at the end of the day those gathered would feast and drink, then would dance or 'hop' around bonfires to the music of local pipers or fiddlers. These gatherings or fairs consequently became known as the 'Hoppings'. Another theory is that the dance performed by the showgirls was called the hop. Most Newcastle people will tell you it rains nearly every year at the Hoppings and local folklore has it that this is a direct result of an old Romany woman's curse. She was apparently thrown off the Town Moor and as a result, in revenge, she laid down a curse that the Hoppings would have bad weather forevermore. In the southeast corner of the Moor is the Newcastle Military Vehicle Museum housed within the last remaining pavilion of the 1929 North East Coast Exhibition.

The Town Moor Hoppings

JESMOND

The leafy suburb of Jesmond has only been part of Newcastle since 1835, but it has been seen as the 'place to live' by the city's inhabitants since the eighteenth century.

Watered by the Ouseburn and its four tributaries, the Cragghall Burn, Moor Crook Letch, Millburn and Sandyford Burn, Jesmond is first recorded in 1204 as 'Gesume', the name probably meaning 'Mouth of the Ouse'. It was always a small settlement and as late as 1801 the population was only 275 but just one hundred years later in 1901, this had increased to over 15,000, with some magnificent houses being built. Amongst these was Jesmond Towers, owned by Charles Mitchell, partner of the local industrialist Lord Armstrong, who built 450 ships on the Tyne.

In 1888-9, he built the Church of St. George with its superb Arts and Crafts decorative interior. The mosaics are simply stunning and it is said local children helped lay them. Mitchell was a dedicated art collector and part of his enlarging of Jesmond Towers included a picture gallery for his collection. The House became La Sagesse School in the 1920s and is still in use as a school today.

Two of the fine houses in Fernwood Road, Thurso House and Kelso House date from 1876 and were merged together in 1912 when Sir Arthur Munro Sutherland left them to the city and they became the city's Mansion House.

Today Jesmond is a very pleasant tree-lined residential area greatly favoured by the city's professionals, academics and business people. There are a

St George's Church, Jesmond

number of good quality schools covering a broad educational spectrum. The focal point of Jesmond seems to revolve around Osborne Road and Acorn Road. Numerous hotels have sprung up over the years along Osborne Road and Jesmond has a growing reputation for its restaurants. Although there are other smaller shopping areas in Jesmond, Acorn Road is probably one of the last remaining shopping streets in a residential area in Newcastle, still retaining something of a village atmosphere.

Being an easy distance from the city on foot or by Metro and with the added advantage of its

two-storied Tyneside Flats, West Jesmond not surprisingly has a considerable student population.

In the 1920's Frederick Charles Pybus, a young surgeon, provided a sparkling energy drink, made from glucose and flavoured with citrus, for his many patients in nursing homes in Jesmond and Gosforth who were recovering from operations. On returning home, his patients went to Owen's pharmacy for further supplies. Realising there was money to be made Owen began making the drink in large quantities and called it Lucozade! The site of the factory is now a university car park.

JESMOND DENE

Jesmond Dene

Jesmond Dene was not always the pleasant narrow wooded valley that follows the Ouseburn between South Gosforth and Jesmond Vale today, providing pleasant walks and a haven for wildlife within Newcastle. Once it was quite industrialised, with quarries and mills and the occasional explosion from a piece of ordnance being tested.

Here lived Lord Armstrong, in a large house, which once stood near the now ruined banqueting hall, where he used to entertain his guests. His explosives and projectiles expert Sir Andrew Noble also lived by the side of the Dene, so it was quite natural for them to test a new gun here in the ravine.

As with Cragside, his marvellous home outside Rothbury, Lord Armstrong and his wife set about changing the valley into a giant garden by planting exotic shrubs and trees and creating miles of footpaths, waterfalls and a grotto. Lady Armstrong split the river into a series of still pools by using weirs and waterfalls and, as at Cragside, boulders were moved and dropped into place to create new features.

In 1883, Lord Armstrong presented the main area of Jesmond Dene to the Corporation of Newcastle upon Tyne for the benefit of its citizens and in 1884, the Prince and Princess of Wales opened the park. In 1950, the council purchased additional land from Lord Armstrong. The Dene has always remained a popular place. Despite the heavy pressures put upon it the Dene retains a peaceful charm of its own. Today the Dene has a Pets' Corner, which is very popular with families and opposite is the Visitor's Centre providing information about Jesmond Dene and its wildlife.

Each Sunday the lovely iron Armstrong Bridge, which crosses the Dene, is awash with artists and craftsmen and craftswomen selling their work. It is said that one of the reasons the bridge was built by Lord Armstrong was to let a local farmer drive his cattle through the park to the low-lying pastures bordering the Ouseburn below. The Armstrong Bridge, closed to road traffic since 1963, is 168 metres long and at its highest point is 19 metres above the Ouseburn.

The Ouseburn continues southwards, blending in with Armstrong Park, Heaton Park and Jesmond Vale, which originally held a settlement for workers in the mines, quarries and brickyards of the area.

NEWCASTLE INTERNATIONAL AIRPORT

Newcastle International Airport started life on 26th July, 1935. The new airport came about as the vision of Sir Stephen Easton, Lord Mayor of the City, who had persuaded the council to invest £35,000 in the project.

At that time the runway was managed by the Newcastle Aero Club and consisted simply of a special type of grass grown from seeds imported from Russia. The terminal as such did not exist and the airport consisted of a small collection of huts.

During the Second World War the Royal Air Force took over the airport and built a wooden control tower positioned on stilts. After the war change came very slowly to the airport with passengers having to use stepladders to get onto the aircraft and having to stand on a set of weighing scales with their luggage when they were checking in. Even the runway lighting was in the form of oil drums that had to be lit by hand.

James Denyer took over the management of the airport in 1952 and a new terminal building was opened in 1967. It is down to his 37 year commitment that the airport is as it is today. To cope with the increased air traffic a new runway was needed, as not only was the old one too short but it was also crumbling. As the new runway is nearly two kilometres long it will take the larger jets, which in turn will increase the number of destinations by attracting new airlines to the region.

A further transformation took place in 1994 when

Newcastle International Airport

the building was upgraded with over 3,200 square metres of glass being used in its construction. The difference this made in the quality of the airport's appearance was astounding. In 2004, with a new £7 million extension giving 3,000 square metres of new space, Newcastle International Airport became the ninth largest airport in the UK. It aims to increase passenger levels to 10 million by 2016.

Today the airport is linked directly with the city by the Metro system, bringing customers and staff to the expanding site. With the airport's growth will come more jobs, more inward investment, more businesses, more tourists, and more wealth for the region. The airport is more than just a transport hub for the region; it is now a focus for wider economic, social and cultural development.

Opposite: Newcastle International Airport

NEWCASTLE RACECOURSE

There has been horse racing in one form or another in the Newcastle area for over 350 years,with records of it at Killingworth in the early seventeenth century. The first mention of Newcastle Races in the common council book is dated 6th August 1695 and at this time the races were run on Killingworth Moor. Racing carried on here until 1721 when the Town Moor became the city's official racing headquarters, although not all the races were as they are today, for example in 1828 a seven-legged horse called Pincushion won two races!

The Town Moor also hosted the first Northumberland Plate, won by Tomboy, in 1833, and continued to do so until the race was transferred to High Gosforth Park in 1881, when the Brandling Estate was purchased for £60,000.

The origin of Newcastle's famous race day at Blaydon is obscure, but they were 'up and running' as it were by 1861, and meetings were held on Whit Mondays and sometimes on August Bank Holiday Mondays. A painting hanging in the Shipley Art Gallery in Gatehead shows the 1862 Blaydon Races, and includes in it all the main people mentioned in George Ridley's famous song. The races ended in 1916 when a two-day meeting ended in a riot after a disputed decision over a horse aptly named Anxious Moments.

The Blaydon Races are now held at Gosforth Park, as is the Beeswing Ladies' Day, named after the most famous horse never to have won the

Newcastle Racecourse at High Gosforth Park

Northumberland Plate. This mare won 46 of her 51 races and produced children and grandchildren, 9 became winners of the Derby, 8 the Oaks, and 11 won the St. Ledger.

Over the years, Gosforth Park has meant many things to Newcastle people besides horse racing. Many of the city's scouts and cubs have spent their first night in a tent at the Scout camp, golfers have driven many a ball along its fairways, squash players have sweated off pounds and birdwatchers have spent long afternoons in the nature reserve.

Over the years, the racecourse fell into decay and Sir Stanley Clarke bought it in 1994. Since that time, £11 million has been invested in High Gosforth Park for sporting and business events, with new facilities, stands, parade rings, and a straight mile track.

BIBLIOGRAPHY

Allsopp, B.	Historical Architecture of Newcastle Upon Tyne,	(Oriel Press Ltd.)
Allsopp, B.	Historical Architecture of Northern England,	(Oriel Press Ltd.)
Ayris, I	A City of Palaces,.	(Newcastle Libraries and Information Service 1997)
Bates, C.J.	History of Northumberland,	(Sandhill Press, reprint 1996)
Bell & Patterson,	Nice Old Time in Newcastle,	(Oriel Press Ltd. 1969)
Bennison, B.	Heady Days, A History of Newcastle's Public Houses,	(Newcastle Libraries and Information Service 1996)
Charlton, R.G.	A History of Newcastle upon Tyne	(W.H. Robinson 1885)
Colls & Lancaster	Newcastle upon Tyne A Modern History,	(Phillimore & Co. Ltd. 2001)
Cullen, F. & Lovie, D.	Newcastle's Grainger Town, An Urban Renaissance,	(English Heritage 2003)
Dobson, H.	City Sights of Newcastle upon Tyne,	(H.G. Dobson 2004)
Dobson, H.	Dobson on Dobson,	(Pentland Press 2000)
Dougan, D.	Newcastle Past and Present,	(Frank Graham)
Faulkener, T., & Greg, A.	John Dobson Architect of the North East,	(Tyne Bridge Publishing 2001)
Fordyce, T.	Local Records or Historical Register of Remarkable Events, Vol. 3 & 4,	(T. Fordyce 1876)
Foster, J.	Newcastle upon Tyne A Pictorial History,	(Phillimore & Co. Ltd).
Graham, F.	Newcastle a Short History & Guide,	(Butler Publishing 1988)
Haws, Duncan	Merchant Fleets, Port Line with Cotty Royden, Tyser & Milburn,	(TCL Publications, Hereford 1990)
Heslop, Jobling & McCombie,	Alderman Fenwick's House	(Society of Antiquaries 2001)
Histon, V.	Ghosts of Grainger Town,	(Tyne Bridge Publishing 2001)
Hobson,	The Ouseburn Valley,	
Hurrell, George	The History of Newcastle General Hospital,	(Hindson & Co Ltd. Reprint 1984)
Joannou, P.	United, The First 100 years,	(Polar Publishing 1994)
Kirkup, M.	The Pitmen's Derby,	(Mid Northumberland Arts Group 1990)
Lancaster,	More Memories of Newcastle upon Tyne,	(True North Books Ltd 1971).
Lancaster, Bill	The Department Store, A Social History,	(Leicester University Press 1995)
Leslie, J & J	Down Our Streets,	(Tyne Bridge Publishing 1993)
Lovie, D.	The Buildings of Grainger Town,	(Grainger Town Partnership, 2001)
MacIvor, I. A	Fortified Frontier	(Tempus Publishing Ltd. 2001)
Mackenzie, E.	A Descriptive & Historical Account of the Town & County of Newcastle upon Tyne	(Mackenzie & Dent 1827)
Manders & Potts,	Crossing The Tyne,	(Tyne Bridge Publishing 2001)
Manders, F.	Cinemas of Newcastle,	(Newcastle Libraries and Arts 1991)
Manders, F.	Newcastle upon Tyne, A Selection of the Earliest Photographs,	(Newcastle Libraries and Arts 1995)
Marshall, W.	Tyne Waters: A River and its Salmon,	(Witherly)
Middlebrook, S.	Newcastle upon Tyne: Its Growth and Achievement,	(Newcastle Chronicle & Journal Ltd. 1950)
Pevsner & Richmond revised Grundy, McCombie, Ryder & Welfare	Buildings of England, Northumberland	(Penguin Books 2001)
Purdue, A. W.	The Ship That Came Home,	(Third Millennium 2003)
Robinson, J. M.	Architecture of Northern England	(Macmillan 1986)
Sykes, J.	Local Records or Historical Register of Remarkable Events, Vol. 1 & 2,	(John Sykes 1866)
The Pybus Society	Medicine in Northumbria, Essays in the history of medicine,	(Alpha Word Power for the Pybus Society, Newcastle upon Tyne 1993)
Underwood, Beach & Morris	Public Sculpture in the Northeast of England,	(Liverpool University Press 2000)
Wilkes, L., & Dodds, G.	Tyneside Classical: The Newcastle of Grainger, Dobson & Clayton,	(John Murray 1964)

Index